Reader's Theater Scripts

Improve Fluency, Vocabulary, and Comprehension

TITLE 1

TEACHER RECOMMENDED · STANDARDS & RESEARCH BASED

Author

Gail Skroback Hennessey, M.S.T.

SHELL EDUCATION

Publishing Credits

Dona Herweck Rice, *Editor-in-Chief*; Lee Aucoin, *Creative Director*; Don Tran, *Print Production Manager*; Conni Medina, M.A.Ed., *Editorial Director*; Jamey Acosta, *Assistant Editor*; Juan Chavolla, *Production Artist*; Corinne Burton, M.S.Ed., *Publisher*

Shell Education

5301 Oceanus Drive
Huntington Beach, CA 92649-1030
http://www.shelleducation.com

ISBN 978-1-4258-0696-5

©2010 Shell Educational Publishing, Inc.
Reprinted 2013

Table of Contents

Introduction

The Connection Between Fluency and Reader's Theater

What Is Reader's Theater?

With reader's theater, students use scripts to practice for a performance. The students do not memorize their lines, and costumes and props are minimal, if used at all. The students convey the meaning of the words using their voices; therefore, interpretation of the text becomes the focus of the activity. Reader's theater gives students at all levels the motivation to practice fluency. The U.S. Department of Education's *Put Reading First* (2001) says: "Reader's theater provides readers with a legitimate reason to reread text and to practice fluency. Reader's theater also promotes cooperative interaction with peers and makes the reading task appealing."

What Is Reading Fluency?

Reading fluency is the ability to read quickly and accurately with meaning, while at the same time using vocal expression (to portray feelings and emotions of characters) and proper phrasing (timing, intonation, word emphasis). The fluent reader groups words in meaningful ways that closely resemble spoken language. Fluency is now seen as a direct connection to reading comprehension (Kuhn and Stahl 2000). It bridges the gap between word recognition and reading comprehension.

The National Reading Panel Report (National Institute of Child Health and Human Development 2000) identified five critical factors that are necessary for effective reading instruction. These factors are:

> ➤ phonemic awareness
> ➤ phonics
> ➤ fluency
> ➤ vocabulary
> ➤ comprehension

Fluency is particularly important for children first learning to read. LaBerge and Samuels (1974) state that readers have a limited amount of attention to focus on reading. Teachers notice this phenomenon when, after listening to a struggling reader, they find that the student cannot explain what he or she has just read. The struggling student has used all available concentration to decode the words and thus fails to grasp the full meaning of the text.

A student who reads fluently processes the text with more comprehension. Timothy Rasinski (1990) found that grouping words into phrases improves comprehension. When the text sounds like natural speech, students are better able to use their own knowledge and experiences to enhance comprehension.

Introduction *(cont.)*

The Connection Between Fluency and Reader's Theater *(cont.)*

How Is Fluency Developed?

Oral reading practice is required for fluency development. Building fluency takes time and develops gradually with practice. A 1979 study by Samuels supports the power of rereading as a fluency builder. In this study, students with learning problems were asked to read a passage several times. Each time the students reread the selection, their reading rate, accuracy, and comprehension increased. The most surprising finding in Samuels's study is that these students also improved on initial readings of other passages of equal or greater difficulty. Their increase in fluency transferred to new and unknown passages.

How Can Reader's Theater Develop Fluency?

Each reader's theater script includes parts for several children to read together, therefore facilitating student participation in a limited form of paired reading, another proven fluency strategy. In paired reading, a stronger reader is partnered with a struggling reader. By listening to the fluent reader, the struggling reader learns how voice, expression, and phrasing help to make sense of the words. This strategy also provides a model for the struggling reader and helps him or her to move through the text at an appropriate rate.

Reader's theater is a simple tool that supports multiple aspects of reading and nets significant gains in reading for the students. It is not only effective in developing reading fluency, it is a motivating factor that can transform a class into eager readers. It is one activity within the school day in which struggling readers do not stand out. With teacher support and repeated practice, all students can do the following:

➤ read their lines with accuracy and expression
➤ gain confidence in their own reading abilities
➤ enhance their listening, vocabulary development, decoding, comprehension, and speaking skills

A Note to Teachers from a Working Teacher

 From the Desk of Cathy Mackey Davis

This book can make a teacher's life easier and provide students with beneficial reading activities. After more than 20 years as an elementary teacher, I thought I'd seen everything come down the reading pike until I received extensive training on the five components of reading. The concept of direct instruction on fluency both surprised and impressed me.

These reader's theater scripts are designed with classroom management in mind. Each reader's theater has assigned roles for students, enabling the teacher to divide the class into small groups, which can be easily monitored. Students can develop fluency through choral reading, an effective strategy that helps students practice their reader's theater parts.

Each script in this book has its own ready-to-use, teacher-friendly lesson plan. The lesson plans cover three key components of reading: vocabulary, comprehension, and fluency. The discussion questions go beyond the literal understanding of a text in an attempt to raise the students' comprehension levels. Graphic organizers are an important part of the lessons, offering direction and bringing closure to the day's activity.

The scripts can also be an addition to classroom Literacy Work Stations. The teacher can place copies of the scripts in a Drama Station or a Fluency Station. Then students choose their parts and practice with minimal teacher intervention. The discussion questions from the lesson plans can be printed on index cards as a part of the station materials. The graphic organizers from the lessons can be enlarged on poster paper as a culminating activity for the stations.

By its very nature, reader's theater encourages students to reread and to use expression and phrasing to convey the meaning of words. It is an activity that both challenges proficient readers and motivates reluctant readers.

Cathy Mackey Davis, M.Ed.
Third Grade Teacher

Introduction *(cont.)*

Differentiation

Classrooms have evolved into diverse pools of learners—English language learners and students performing above grade level, below grade level, and on grade level. Teachers are expected to meet the diverse needs of all students in one classroom. Differentiation encompasses what is taught, how it is taught, and the products children create to show what they have learned. These categories are often referred to as content, process, and product. Teachers can keep these categories in mind as they plan instruction that will best meet the needs of their students.

Differentiating for Below-Grade-Level Students

Below-grade-level students will need help with complex concepts. They need concrete examples and models to help with comprehension. They may also need extra guidance in developing oral and written language. By receiving extra support and understanding, these students will feel more secure and have greater success.

- ➤ Model fluent reading before asking students to practice on their own.
- ➤ Allocate extra practice time for oral language activities.
- ➤ Allow for kinesthetic (hands-on) activities where appropriate. For example, students may act out the meaning of a vocabulary word.

Differentiating for Above-Grade-Level Students

All students need a firm foundation in the key vocabulary and concepts of the curriculum. Even above-grade-level students may not know much about these words or concepts before a lesson begins. The difference is that they usually learn the concepts quickly. The activities and end products can be adapted appropriately for individual students.

- ➤ Ask students to explain their reasoning for their decisions about phrasing, intonation, and expression.
- ➤ Have students design their own reader's theater scripts.

Differentiating for English Language Learners

Like all learners, English language learners need teachers who have a strong knowledge base and are committed to developing students' language. It is crucial that teachers work carefully to develop English language learners' academic vocabularies. Teachers of English language learners should keep in mind the following important principles:

- ➤ Make use of realia, concrete materials, visuals, pantomime, and other nonlinguistic representations of concepts to make input comprehensible.
- ➤ Ensure that students have ample opportunities for social interactions.
- ➤ Create a nonthreatening atmosphere that encourages students to use their new language.
- ➤ Introduce words in rich contexts that support meaning.
- ➤ Respect and draw on students' backgrounds and experiences and build connections between the known and the new.

Introduction *(cont.)*

How to Use This Book

This book includes 12 reader's theater scripts and grade-level-appropriate lessons. Within each focused lesson you will find suggestions for how to connect the script to a piece of literature and a specific content area; a vocabulary mini-lesson; activities for before, during, and after reading the script; and written and oral response questions.

Literature Connection

Content Connection

Vocabulary Activity

Before the Reader's Theater

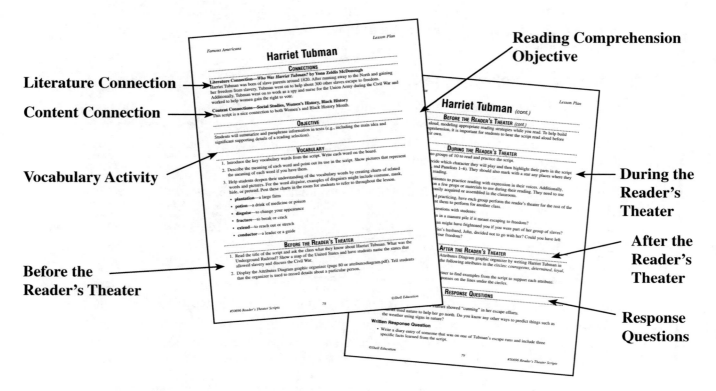

Reading Comprehension Objective

During the Reader's Theater

After the Reader's Theater

Response Questions

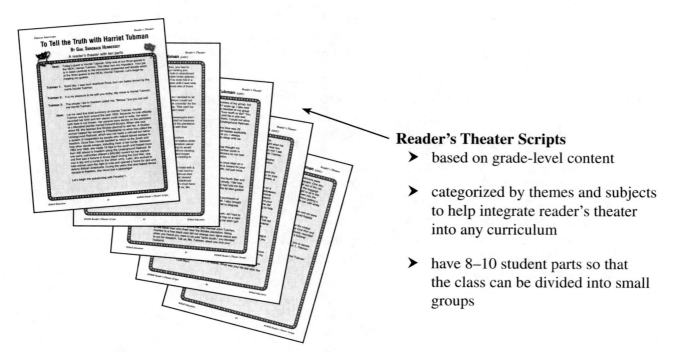

Reader's Theater Scripts

➤ based on grade-level content

➤ categorized by themes and subjects to help integrate reader's theater into any curriculum

➤ have 8–10 student parts so that the class can be divided into small groups

Introduction *(cont.)*

How to Use This Book *(cont.)*

Each lesson introduces a specific graphic organizer. A reproducible copy of each graphic organizer is provided in the lesson. Additionally, a PDF of each graphic organizer is available on the Teacher Resource CD.

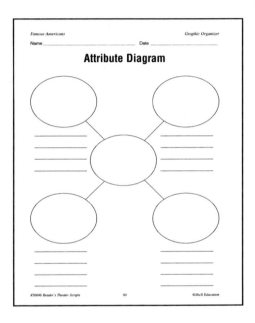

Suggestions for Using and Displaying the Graphic Organizer

➤ **Make a transparency** of the graphic organizer and use it as a model during the lesson.

➤ **Use chart paper** to recreate the graphic organizer. Complete the graphic organizer as you teach the lesson.

➤ **Use the electronic copy** of the graphic organizer from the Teacher Resource CD to project onto the board or an interactive whiteboard.

Contents of the Teacher Resource CD

➤ PDF of each graphic organizer

➤ PDF of each script

➤ The contents of the CD are listed on page 102.

Introduction *(cont.)*

Standards Correlations

Shell Education is committed to producing educational materials that are research and standards based. In this effort, we have correlated all of our products to the academic standards of all 50 states, the District of Columbia, and the Department of Defense Dependent Schools.

How to Find Standards Correlations

To print a customized correlation report of this product for your state, visit our website at **www.shelleducation.com** and follow the on-screen directions. If you require assistance in printing correlation reports, please contact Customer Service at 1-877-777-3450.

Purpose and Intent of Standards

The No Child Left Behind legislation mandates that all states adopt academic standards that identify the skills students will learn in kindergarten through grade twelve. While many states had already adopted academic standards prior to NCLB, the legislation set requirements to ensure the standards were detailed and comprehensive.

Standards are designed to focus instruction and guide adoption of curricula. Standards are statements that describe the criteria necessary for students to meet specific academic goals. They define the knowledge, skills, and content students should acquire at each level. Standards are also used to develop standardized tests to evaluate students' academic progress.

Teachers are required to demonstrate how their lessons meet state standards. State standards are used in development of all of our products, so educators can be assured they meet the academic requirements of each state.

McREL Compendium

We use the Mid-continent Research for Education and Learning (McREL) Compendium to create standards correlations. Each year, McREL analyzes state standards and revises the compendium. By following this procedure, McREL is able to produce a general compilation of national standards. Each lesson in this product is based on one or more McREL standards. The chart on the following pages lists each standard taught in this product and the corresponding lessons.

Introduction *(cont.)*

Standards Correlations Chart

Language Arts Standards	
Lesson Title	**McREL Standard**
Socrates	Students will reflect on what has been learned after reading and formulate ideas, opinions, and personal responses to texts.
Archimedes	Students will differentiate between fact and opinion in informational texts.
Hannibal	Students will use reading skills and strategies to understand a variety of informational texts (e.g., textbooks; biographical sketches; essays).
Alexander the Great	Students will summarize and paraphrase information in texts (e.g., arrange information in sequential order; convey main ideas, critical details, and underlying meaning).
Leonardo da Vinci	Students will summarize and paraphrase information in texts (e.g., arrange information in sequential order; convey main ideas, critical details, and underlying meaning).
Louis Braille	Students will summarize and paraphrase information in texts (e.g., arrange information in sequential order; convey main ideas, critical details, and underlying meaning).
Elizabeth Blackwell	Students will summarize and paraphrase information in texts (e.g., arrange information in sequential order; convey main ideas, critical details, and underlying meaning).
Gandhi	Students will summarize and paraphrase information in texts (e.g., arrange information in sequential order; convey main ideas, critical details, and underlying meaning).
Edgar Allan Poe	Students will summarize and paraphrase information in texts (e.g., arrange information in sequential order; convey main ideas, critical details, and underlying meaning).
Harriet Tubman	Students will use reading skills and strategies to understand a variety of informational texts (e.g., textbooks; biographical sketches; essays).
Emily Dickinson	Students will use reading skills and strategies to understand a variety of informational texts (e.g., textbooks; biographical sketches; essays).
Mark Twain	Students will use reading skills and strategies to understand a variety of informational texts (e.g., textbooks; biographical sketches; essays).

Introduction *(cont.)*

Standards Correlations Chart *(cont.)*

Vocabulary Standards	
Lesson Title	**McREL Standard**
All scripts	Uses level-appropriate vocabulary in speech (e.g., metaphorical language, specialized language, sensory details).
All scripts	Uses a variety of strategies to extend reading vocabulary (e.g., uses definition, restatement, example, comparison and contrast to verify word meanings; knows vocabulary related to different content areas and current events).

Fluency Standards	
Lesson Title	**McREL Standard**
All scripts	Uses appropriate verbal and nonverbal techniques for oral presentations (e.g., inflection/modulation of voice, tempo, word choice, feeling, expression, tone, volume, enunciation, physical gestures, body movement, eye contact, posture).
All scripts	Understands elements of persuasion and appeal in spoken texts (e.g., purpose and impact of pace, volume, tone, stress, music; images and ideas conveyed by vocabulary).

Introduction (cont.)

Tips on Reader's Theater

By Aaron Shepard

Mumble, mumble,
Stop and stumble.
Pages turn and readers fumble.

If this sounds like a description of your reader's theater efforts, try giving your readers the following tips. First, have your readers follow these instructions—individually or in a group—to prepare their scripts and get familiar with their parts.

Preparing	• Highlight your parts in your copy of the script. Mark only the words you will say—not your character's name or stage directions. • Underline the words that tell about anything you'll need to act out. • Read through your part aloud. If you're a character, think about how that character would sound. How does your character feel? Can you speak as if you were feeling that way? • Stand up and read through the script again. If you're a character, try out faces and movements. Would your character stand or move in a special way? Can you do that?
Rehearsing	• Hold your script at a steady height, but make sure it doesn't hide your face. • Speak with feeling. • S-l-o-w d-o-w-n. Say each syl-la-ble clear-ly. • TALK LOUDLY! You have to be heard in the back row. • While you speak, try to look up often. Don't just look at your script. • The narrators are important even when the audience isn't looking at you. You control the story! Be sure to give the characters enough time to do what they must. And remember that you're talking to the audience, not to yourself. • Characters, you give the story life! Remember to be your character even when you're not speaking, and be sure to react to the other characters.
Performing	• If the audience laughs, stop speaking until they can hear you again. • If someone talks in the audience, don't pay attention. • If someone walks into the room, don't look at them. • If you make a mistake, pretend it was right. • If a reader forgets to read his or her part, don't signal to the reader, just skip over it or make something up.

Socrates

CONNECTIONS

Literature Connection—*Wise Guy: The Life and Philosophy of Socrates* by M. D. Usher

This fiction book tells a kid-friendly story about Socrates. Born in ancient Greece in 469 B.C., Socrates is remembered as one of the greatest philosophers of his day. He spent his life searching for knowledge and truth. He died defending a new idea, called trial by jury, and is credited for developing a learning technique that involves questioning. This book is a great way to introduce the many complexities within philosophy.

Content Connections—World Cultures

This script would be a nice connection to a study on ancient cultures of the world or a lesson on trial by jury.

OBJECTIVE

Students will reflect on what has been learned after reading and formulate ideas, opinions, and personal responses to texts.

VOCABULARY

1. Introduce the key vocabulary words from the script. Write each word on the board. Read each of the vocabulary words aloud and ask students to speculate on the meaning of each word.

2. Describe the meaning of each word and point out its use in the script.

3. Ask students to write a short story, using all six vocabulary words.

   - **philosopher**—a person who loves learning and searching for truth
   - **bulging**—sticking out
   - **quench**—to satisfy your thirst
   - **tradition**—a custom or way of doing something
   - **corrupting**—lowering character or moral standards
   - **criticism**—the act of finding fault in someone or something

BEFORE THE READER'S THEATER

1. Read the title of the script. Ask students to make predictions about the selection based on the title. What will this script be about? What do students know about Socrates?

2. Display the K-W-L Chart graphic organizer (page 16 or kwlchart.pdf). Explain to students that this type of graphic organizer will help to categorize the information they know, want to know, and (after reading the script) have learned about Socrates and the country of Greece.

3. Demonstrate its use by filling out a few examples of prior knowledge about Socrates under the "K" column of the K-W-L Chart. Ask questions such as, "What do you know about the country of Greece?"

Socrates *(cont.)*

BEFORE THE READER'S THEATER *(cont.)*

4. Complete the "W" column by asking questions, such as "What do you want to know about Socrates? What types of things would you like to learn about the country of Greece?"

5. Explain that the class will complete the last column of the chart ("L") after reading the script.

6. Read the script aloud, modeling appropriate reading strategies while you read. To help build fluency and comprehension, it is important for students to hear the script read aloud before practicing on their own.

DURING THE READER'S THEATER

1. Divide the class into groups of seven to read and practice the script.

2. Students need to decide which character they will play and then highlight their parts in the script (Socrates 1–3, Panelists 1–3, and Host). They should also mark with a star any places where they need to pause while reading.

3. Give students a few minutes to practice reading with expression in their voices. Additionally, students may decide on a few props or materials to use during their reading. They need to use materials that can be easily acquired or assembled in the classroom.

4. After they have finished practicing, have each group perform the reader's theater for the rest of the class. You may also want them to perform for another class.

5. Ask students if they know the answer to the question "Who is the REAL Socrates?" (**Note:** The REAL Socrates is Socrates 1.)

AFTER THE READER'S THEATER

1. As a class, fill in the information in the "L" column of the K-W-L Chart.

2. Have students conduct organized research about Socrates and Greece using a variety of sources, including reference books, magazines, encyclopedias, and the Internet.

3. After gathering sufficient information, students will write a report sharing their findings. Make sure students list the sources of information they used.

RESPONSE QUESTIONS

Group Discussion Questions

- A philosopher is a person who loves to learn. Can you think of any famous people who might be modern day "philosophers"?

- Ancient people of the world believed in many gods. Why did they worship things in nature and why was the sun god so important?

Written Response Question

- Why do you think Socrates took poison if he didn't believe he had done anything wrong?

Name_____ Date _____

K-W-L Chart

K	W	L

To Tell the Truth with Socrates

By Gail Skroback Hennessey

A reader's theater with seven parts

Host: Today's guest is Socrates. Only one of our three guests is the REAL philosopher of ancient Greece. The other two are imposters. Your job is to listen carefully to the information presented and decide which of the three guests is the REAL Socrates. Let's begin by meeting our guests:

Socrates 1: Hello, my name is Socrates.

Socrates 2: Good day, students, I am Socrates.

Socrates 3: It is an honor to be with you. My name is Socrates.

Host: Let me read this brief summary on Socrates. Socrates was born in ancient Greece around the year 469 B.C. Socrates is remembered as one of the greatest philosophers of all time. He spent his life in the pursuit of knowledge and in the search for truth. Socrates believed that no one willingly did evil. Individuals only did wrong because they were ignorant and only needed knowledge to know how to be good. He is credited with developing the Socratic Method, a learning process that uses questions to develop an idea or obtain an answer. The Socratic method revealed people's ignorance by showing that many ideas thought to be true were actually false. Unfortunately, many citizens of ancient Athens distrusted Socrates and disagreed with his beliefs. In 399 B.C., he was put on trial for some of his beliefs. He was convicted and sentenced to death.

Let's begin the questioning with Panelist 1.

Panelist 1: You were a stonecutter's son who was educated in the basic subjects that the people of Athens thought important. You studied music to train your mind and participated in sports and physical conditioning to train your body. You also learned math and read and recited such works as Homer's *Iliad* and *Odyssey*. Tell us, Socrates, about a memory from your childhood.

To Tell the Truth with Socrates *(cont.)*

Socrates 1: After seeing my disappointing attempts at stonecutting, my father decided that I would never be a good stonecutter. He said that marble was too expensive to be wasted. When he told me that stone figures, such as a lion, were waiting to be set free from the marble by the stonecutter, I thought of the many ideas that were waiting to be set free by someone who asked the correct questions.

Socrates 2: I often got what I called a "funny feeling" and thought of it as a divine sign. I learned to depend on these feelings whenever I needed to work out a problem or find an answer.

Socrates 3: I did not like taking the gods' names lightly, so instead of saying the common phrase, "By Zeus," I used the phrase, "By the Dog of Egypt," whenever I wished to make a strong remark.

Panelist 2: Socrates, please describe yourself to us.

Socrates 1: I had bulging eyes, thick lips, and a stubby nose. Children called me "frog face." I had my share of fights over this nickname.

Socrates 2: Since I was not very handsome, I tried to focus on the good things about my features. My stubby nose allowed me to sniff the air for smells better and my bulging eyes enabled me to see in all directions.

Socrates 3: Even as a child I looked for the meaning of things. I once told my father that a beautiful pitcher was nothing but an arrangement of clay; it was its use that gave it beauty. I did pray to Zeus, our chief god, to make me beautiful on the inside, since I was so plain looking on the outside.

Panelist 3: As a citizen of Athens, you participated in the wars against Sparta, now called the Peloponnesian Wars (432–429 B.C.). One day, you rescued your friend, Alcibiades, who was wounded in battle and took him to safety. You refused an award for your bravery. Socrates, tell us something else about yourself.

To Tell the Truth with Socrates *(cont.)*

Socrates 1: Well, I tried never to show hatred or anger toward others. One day, in the heat of a discussion, a companion slapped me. When I jokingly responded, "It's annoying not knowing when to put on a helmet before going out," he got even angrier.

Socrates 2: I loved to draw and always carried a packet of markers in my back pocket. The Athenian Gazette published my colored drawings of battle scenes in its daily edition.

Socrates 3: I loved music and became very good at playing the banjo that I always kept near. One day, when returning to camp after a battle near a place called Alabama, I started to hum a tune that has become quite famous. I'm sure you've heard it. It begins, "Oh, Susanna, don't you cry for me..."

Panelist 1: You spent your day in the Agora, or main public square, of Athens. You walked among the people there, chatting, questioning, and thinking about the problems of the day. You never held a job and did not take money for your teaching. You wanted to learn from those with whom you worked. You claimed that you were different from others because you KNEW that you were ignorant. What did your wife, Xanthippe, think of your reputation in Athens as a man who desired knowledge?

Socrates 1: Sadly, my wife was not proud of me and she always found fault with me, saying that I should get a job! One day, she even threw a jug of water in my face. She was also known to throw furniture!

Socrates 2: My wife was very proud to be married to such a respected thinker like me.

Socrates 3: My wife kept a notebook of all the things I learned and created a board game called "Trivial Pursuit" that made us rich!

Panelist 2: You were eventually arrested for corrupting young minds and being disrespectful to the religious traditions of the time. You were found guilty and sentenced to die by drinking poison hemlock. Although you had many opportunities to escape from jail, you did not. Why did you so willingly accept your fate and take the poison?

To Tell the Truth with Socrates *(cont.)*

Socrates 1: I accepted my fate because a jury of my peers (more than 500 citizens), chosen by lot, found me guilty. I believed that trial by jury, a gift of the ancient Greeks to the people of today, was a good idea. Although I did not agree with the jury's decision, I respected the trial by jury system and I believed it was my duty to obey their decision.

Socrates 2: To be honest, I did not take the poison willingly. It was very hot in my jail cell and the jailer asked if I would like something to quench my thirst. Unknown to me, he had placed the poison hemlock in the watermelon punch he gave me to drink!

Socrates 3: As was stated earlier, my wife was very difficult to live with. I chose the poison over the possibility that the jury would change my punishment to house arrest!

Panelist 3: You are quoted as saying, "The unexamined life is not worth living." You also lived by the quote, "Know thyself," words carved into the cornerstone of the Temple of Apollo at Delphi. Socrates, please share another belief by which you lived.

Socrates 1: I especially liked, "The best and easiest way to stop criticism is to make yourself as good as you can."

Socrates 2: I liked to tell the young boys who played sports that "any method is acceptable as long as you WIN!"

Socrates 3: I remember telling my students, "Sticks and stones may break your bones, but names can never hurt you."

Host: Panelists and members of the audience, it is now time for you to decide which of our guests is the REAL Socrates. Is it Socrates 1, Socrates 2, or Socrates 3?

All right, the votes have been cast. Will the REAL Socrates please stand up?

Archimedes

CONNECTIONS

Literature Connections—*Archimedes and the Door of Science* by Jeanne Bendrick
This is a wonderful book for young readers. It tells the story of Archimedes, a great mathematician, engineer, and physicist. Born around 287 B.C., he is remembered for being one of the first people to use experiments to test ideas.

Content Connections—Social Studies, Ancient Cultures
This script would connect well with studies on ancient cultures, in science with the study of buoyancy, and even math when logic is discussed.

OBJECTIVE

Students will differentiate between fact and opinion in informational texts.

VOCABULARY

1. Introduce the key vocabulary words from the script. Write each word on the board. Read each word aloud.

2. Describe the meaning of each word and point out its use in the script.

3. Challenge the class to a game of team charades. Divide the class into small groups. Assign each group a vocabulary word to act out for the class. Give each group three minutes to decide how to demonstrate its assigned word. Challenge the other groups to guess the word.

   - **calculate**—to figure out or compute

   - **physicist**—a scientist who studies matter and energy

   - **desperate**—almost hopeless

   - **diagram**—a sketch, drawing, or plan

   - **device**—an invention or something constructed

   - **mythology**—stories about gods, goddesses, and ancestors

BEFORE THE READER'S THEATER

1. Read the title of the script and ask the class if they have ever heard of Archimedes. Do they know where Greece is on a map? Can they state three facts about Greece?

2. Read the script aloud, modeling appropriate reading strategies while you read. To help build fluency and comprehension, it is important for students to hear the script read aloud before practicing on their own.

Archimedes (cont.)

DURING THE READER'S THEATER

1. Divide the class into groups of nine to read and practice the script.

2. Students need to decide which character they will play and then highlight their parts in the script (Archimedes 1–3, Host, and Panelists 1–5). They should also mark with a star any places where they need to pause while reading.

3. Give students a few minutes to practice reading with expression in their voices. Additionally, students may decide on a few props or materials to use during their reading. They need to use materials that can be easily acquired or assembled in the classroom.

4. After they have finished practicing, have each group perform the reader's theater for the rest of the class. You may also want them to perform for another class.

5. Ask students if they know the answer to the question "Who is the REAL Archimedes?" (**Note:** The REAL Archimedes is Archimedes 2.)

6. Discuss the following questions with students:

   • What are several things that people have used as "paper" over the years?

   • Have you ever done something that caused you embarrassment?

   • What do you think the king did to the goldsmith who cheated him?

AFTER THE READER'S THEATER

1. Display the Fact or Opinion graphic organizer (page 23 or factoropinion.pdf).

2. After reading the script, have students list factual statements about Archimedes and statements about Archimedes that are opinions.

3. Discuss why each statement is an opinion or a fact and demonstrate how changing a word or two can change a fact to an opinion and vice versa.

4. Have students complete the graphic organizer as a class, independently, or in pairs.

RESPONSE QUESTIONS

Group Discussion Questions

• Can you name two things that Archimedes is credited with doing?

• Do you think it was easier to become an "educated" person in the past or is it easier today?

Written Response Question

• Pretend to be Archimedes and write a diary entry detailing your discovery regarding the king's crown.

Name _____   Date _____

Fact	Opinion

To Tell the Truth with Archimedes

By Gail Skroback Hennessey

A reader's theater with nine parts

Host: Today's guest is Archimedes. Only one of our three guests is the REAL Greek mathematician, Archimedes. The other two are imposters. Your job is to listen carefully to the information presented and decide which of the three guests is the REAL Archimedes. Let's begin by meeting our guests.

Archimedes 1: Good day, students! My name is Archimedes

Archimedes 2: Greetings, everyone! My name is Archimedes.

Archimedes 3: Archimedes is my name and I am glad that I came!

Host: Let me read this brief summary on Archimedes. Archimedes was born around the year 287 B.C. in the city of Syracuse, on the island of Sicily, which was then part of the Greek empire. Although he is famous for his many inventions, he actually considered inventing as a way to relax! His real love was mathematics, and he was an engineer and a physicist, too. Some call him the "father of experimental science" because he tested all his ideas with experiments. He is credited with discovering the laws of the lever and the pulley, a simple machine that lifted heavy loads. He is also credited with developing a branch of physics called hydrostatics that deals with the basic laws of fluids, such as the law of buoyancy.

For fun, he enjoyed doing brainteasers, such as calculating the grains of sand necessary to fill the universe or estimating the distance between Earth and the sun.

During his life, the Romans fought with the Greeks for possession of Sicily. In 212 B.C., the Romans succeeded in taking the city of Syracuse on Sicily. At the time, Archimedes was working at home on an experiment when a Roman soldier entered his house. Although the Roman leader, Marcellus, had ordered soldiers to spare Archimedes' life, the soldier killed him with his sword. Marcellus was so upset about Archimedes' death that he built a statue in the mathematician's honor!

Let's begin the questioning with Panelist 1.

To Tell the Truth with Archimedes *(cont.)*

Panelist 1: Learning was important in your family. In fact, your father was a famous astronomer who calculated the diameters of the sun and moon. Tell us about your schooling.

Archimedes 1: In school, I learned math, writing, reading, geography, and music. I wrote on wooden boards covered with wax because only children older than eight were allowed to write on papyrus paper for their assignments.

Archimedes 2: I traveled to Alexandria, Egypt to study at the city's library, which had more than one million papyrus books!

Archimedes 3: I especially liked the subject of mathematics and read many books written by the Greek mathematician, Euclid, often called the "father of mathematics."

Panelist 2: You spent your life in Syracuse, Sicily, and quickly became known to Hieron, the king of Syracuse. He built a large ship, but when it came time to move it, the boat was too heavy to budge! King Hieron asked for your mathematical help to launch the ship that he feared only an army of men could move. So you invented a giant lever, a simple machine that lifted the ship and allowed it to be launched. The king was so pleased that he declared, "From this day forward, Archimedes will be believed, no matter what he says." Tell us more about yourself, Archimedes.

Archimedes 1: I really enjoyed experimenting with pulleys and levers. In fact, once I got involved in a project, I often forgot to eat! My discoveries led to the invention of machines that could move heavy loads, so I once said, "Give me a spot where I can stand and I can move Earth!"

Archimedes 2: I became very well known because of my work and was nicknamed "Alpha," which is the first letter of the Greek alphabet. I was thought to be the most educated person of my time, or the "first" in knowledge.

To Tell the Truth with Archimedes *(cont.)*

Archimedes 3: When I got an idea, I recorded my thoughts on whatever I could find. Often, I used the earth as my chalkboard. I also drew my ideas in the ashes of a fire. When desperate, I was known to oil my skin and draw on my body. Even taking a bath did not stop my thinking. I would simply draw diagrams of my ideas on my wet skin!

Panelist 3: You devised a number system called "order numbers," which is still used today to write very large numbers. You invented the Archimedean screw, a device that raises water, which is still used today to irrigate crops in Egypt! You also developed a formula to find the volume of a sphere and found a more accurate value for pi, the ratio of the circumference of a circle to its diameter. Perhaps your most famous mathematical discovery was for King Hieron. Hieron thought a goldsmith had cheated him by making a new crown that was not pure gold. Tell us how you proved whether the crown was pure gold.

Archimedes 1: To be honest, I did not need my mathematical mind to figure out this puzzle. Since the goldsmith knew I could use my brilliant mind to figure out whether he had cheated the king, he offered me a bribe of a beautiful solid gold watch if I told the king that the crown was pure gold. Remember, the king had declared to all that whatever I said must be accepted as true. Since my neon orange watch had just stopped working, I agreed to say the crown was pure gold and went home with a beautiful new watch.

Archimedes 2: I did a lot of thinking while in the bathtub! One day, as I stepped into the tub, I noticed that some of the water spilled out over the top. That observation gave me an idea about how to determine whether the crown was solid gold. Since different metals displace different amounts of water, I decided to measure the amount of water displaced by a specific mass of solid gold. If the goldsmith had added silver to the gold mixture when making the crown, then the amount of water displaced would be different from the amount of water displaced by the same amount of pure gold. I was so excited about my discovery that I got out of the tub and ran down the street yelling, "Eureka, I have found it!" Unfortunately, I forgot to put on my clothes before I ran into the street! It was a bit embarrassing!

To Tell the Truth with Archimedes *(cont.)*

Archimedes 3: I developed a theory that enabled me to figure out the weight of gold inside the crown. My theory was called the Theory of Relativity. It involved showing the crown, which the king allowed me to borrow, to FIVE of my relatives. Each relative was asked to hold the crown and determine if it looked like it was made of solid gold. If the majority of my five relatives said that it was gold, then it was gold. Based on my Theory of Relativity, the crown was NOT pure gold and the king punished the goldsmith for cheating!

Panelist 4: When the Romans attacked the city of Syracuse in 215 B.C., they did not realize that it would take several years to win the war. You were very important in holding off the Romans, because you invented a catapult that flung rocks at their ships. You also developed a device that had huge iron hooks that could lift their boats into the air and drop them crashing into the sea. Did you invent any other weapons to be used against the Romans?

Archimedes 1: You may have read that David Bushnell invented the first submarine during the Revolutionary War, from 1775 to 1783, and called it the Turtle. This is not correct. Back in 213 B.C., I invented a submarine, which was powered by solar energy cells located on the top of the submarine. Our soldiers were able to sneak up to the Roman ships in the harbor and torpedo them out of the waters! By the way, my first submarine was called the Tadpole.

Archimedes 2: One of my most unique weapons developed to fight the Romans involved using a giant mirror that reflected the sun's rays on the Roman ships, causing them to burst into flames.

Archimedes 3: I was very proud of an invention I called a cloaking device. When the machine was running, anything caught within its beam of light became invisible. This enabled our soldiers to creep close to the Roman ships without being seen and destroy them before they knew what hit them!

To Tell the Truth with Archimedes *(cont.)*

Panelist 5: Although you helped to prevent the Roman leader, Marcellus, from seizing Syracuse for almost three years, he greatly respected your brilliant mind. He called you "Briareus," a Greek mythological creature with 100 arms, and warned his soldiers to not harm you. How did you die?

Archimedes 1: A Roman soldier barged into my home one afternoon and started to insult me. It angered me that he did not appreciate my talent or respect me for the great mathematician that I was. I used my sword to fight a duel with him, but, unfortunately, I lost.

Archimedes 2: As you know, I drew many diagrams on the dirt floor of my house. A Roman soldier entered my home and stepped all over my current work. I told him to watch where he was walking; he got angry, drew his sword and killed me.

Archimedes 3: Did you ever hear the expression, "It's a small world?" Well, it turns out that the Roman soldier who entered my house was the son of the goldsmith who had cheated the king years ago. He killed me because I proved the goldsmith cheated and he blamed me because the king sent his father to prison where he died making license plates.

Host: Panelists and members of the audience, it is now time for you to decide which of our guests is the REAL Archimedes. Is it Archimedes 1, Archimedes 2, or Archimedesr 3?

All right, the votes have been cast. Will the REAL Archimedes please stand up?

Hannibal

CONNECTIONS

Literature Connection—*Hannibal: Rome's Worst Nightmare* by Philip Brooks
This book details the life of Hannibal, one of the greatest generals in history. He is remembered for his military strategies and leadership even though he lost his battles against the Romans.

Content Connections—Ancient Cultures
This script would be a nice connection to a study on ancient cultures of the world.

OBJECTIVE

Students will use reading skills and strategies to understand a variety of informational texts (e.g., textbooks; biographical sketches; essays).

VOCABULARY

1. Write the vocabulary words on the board and discuss the definitions.

2. Have the students determine the part of speech for each vocabulary word by looking up information in the dictionary, if necessary.

3. Students should write each of the vocabulary words in a sentence.

   • **devised**—figured out a plan

   • **strategies**—methods used to achieve a goal

   • **capsize**—to over turn

   • **avalanche**—a mass of snow that slides down a mountainside

   • **phrase**—a brief expression consisting of several words

BEFORE THE READER'S THEATER

1. Read the title of the script. Ask students to make predictions about the selection. Then ask the class if they have ever heard of Hannibal.

2. Display the Question Strips graphic organizer (page 31 or questionstrips.pdf). Provide each student with a copy. Each reader's theater group will write one question for each strip after practicing the script.

3. Read the script aloud, modeling appropriate reading strategies while you read. To help build fluency and comprehension, it is important for students to hear the script read aloud before practicing on their own.

Hannibal *(cont.)*

DURING THE READER'S THEATER

1. Divide the class into groups of nine to read and practice the script.

2. Students need to decide which character they will play and then highlight their parts in the script (Hannibal 1–3, Host, and Panelists 1–5). They should also mark with a star any places where they need to pause while reading.

3. Give students a few minutes to practice reading with expression in their voices. Additionally, students may decide on a few props or materials to use during their reading. They need to use materials that can be easily acquired or assembled in the classroom.

4. After they have finished practicing, have each group perform the reader's theater for the rest of the class. You may also want them to perform for another class.

5. Ask students if they know the answer to the question "Who is the REAL Hannibal?" (**Note:** The REAL Hannibal is Hannibal 1.)

6. Discuss the following questions with students:

   • Do you think because Hannibal treated himself like the rest of his soldiers, that he was more or less respected by his men?

   • What do you think Hannibal thought of women by his comment, "Shade is for women"?

   • Why do you think countries wanted to control the Mediterranean Sea?

AFTER THE READER'S THEATER

1. After practicing the script, have the groups work together to complete the Question Strips graphic organizer. Tell students that after they write the questions, they should record their answers on a separate piece of paper.

2. Bring the class back together and have each group share their questions and answers.

3. Have students find other books about Hannibal that they would be interested in reading.

RESPONSE QUESTIONS

Group Discussion Questions

• Name three characteristics of Hannibal and provide three examples from the script as support.

• Hannibal used elephants in war. Do you know of any other animals that have been used in war?

Written Response Question

• Write a diary about a day in your life pretending to be Hannibal. Include three specific facts about Hannibal learned from the script.

Name_____   Date _____

Question Strips

Who?	_____

What?	_____

When?	_____

Why?	_____

How?	_____

What If?	_____

To Tell the Truth with Hannibal
BY GAIL SKROBACK HENNESSEY
A reader's theater with nine parts

Host: Today's guest is Hannibal Barca. Only one of our three guests is the REAL Hannibal. The other two are imposters. Your job is to listen carefully to the information presented and decide which of the three guests is the REAL Hannibal. Let's begin by meeting our guests.

Hannibal 1: Greetings! I'm the greatest general in history. I'm Hannibal!

Hannibal 2: Hannibal, Hannibal, that's my name. Fighting in wars, that's my fame!

Hannibal 3: Good day to you all. My name is Hannibal of ancient Carthage.

Host: Let me read this brief summary on Hannibal. Hannibal Barca was born in 247 B.C. in Carthage, an ancient North African city. His father was a military leader who made Hannibal, when he was only about nine years old, promise to always be an enemy of Rome. When the Second Punic War began between Carthage and the city of Rome, Hannibal commanded the military forces and devised a clever plan to conquer the Romans. However, even after 15 years of battle and many victories over the Romans, Hannibal was unable to conquer the city of Rome. Although he was not successful in conquering the Romans, he is remembered as one of the greatest generals in history for his creative military strategies and strong leadership.

Let's begin the questioning with Panelist 1.

Panelist 1: You were the military leader during the second Punic War between Rome and Carthage—a series of wars that lasted nearly 118 years. Both powerful cities were fighting for control of the Mediterranean Sea and, specifically, the island of Sicily. The Punic Wars got their name because the Latin name for Carthage is Punicus, meaning Phoenician—the people who first established the city on the coast of northern Africa. Tell us, as a military leader, what were you like?

To Tell the Truth with Hannibal *(cont.)*

Hannibal 1: I learned from my father never to submit to Roman rule. In fact, that was my most important lesson and it was repeated many times by my father and my tutors. But I was also an educated man. I learned about Greek philosophers and the poems of the great Greek poet Homer. I loved reading accounts of history and Greek science and put the knowledge I gained to use in my military career.

Hannibal 2: Even at the young age of five, I remember spending time at my father's military camps where I learned the customs, superstitions, and languages of the different soldiers. I learned that a great leader must unite all the people within his army and must not act superior to his men.

Hannibal 3: I dressed like a common soldier, slept on the ground, and was usually the first to enter a battle and the last to leave. By the way, the Second Punic War, in which I fought, was called the "World War of Ancient Times."

Panelist 2: Many historical figures are remembered for having said something significant. Would you share with us something you once said?

Hannibal 1: Well, I once said, "Shade is for women!"

Hannibal 2: Hmmm, I remember saying, "A thinking man is least alone when by himself." And, yes, I was a loner!

Hannibal 3: I was not much of a talker, I preferred to listen and to learn, but I did have a thought about battle: "War is the supreme exercise of intelligence."

Panelist 3: Many interesting things must have happened to you during your long career as a soldier. Please share some of these experiences.

Hannibal 1: Well, if you haven't noticed, I can only see out of one eye. It happened during our march through the Arno River. There was nowhere to sleep in the swampy marsh in which we found ourselves. Mosquitoes were everywhere breeding disease! I used one of the elephants that had died as a cot to sleep on above the swamp to protect myself! Unfortunately, I got an eye infection anyway and lost sight in one eye.

To Tell the Truth with Hannibal *(cont.)*

Hannibal 2:　As we crossed the Alps, a winter blizzard began causing an avalanche! Boulders blocked the only pathway. Drawing from my scientific knowledge, I ordered the men to place logs and tree trunks by the boulders and to set them on fire to heat the rocks. The wine the men carried in containers was old and had turned to vinegar, so I ordered them to pour it onto the heated rocks. My men thought it was magic when, after repeated efforts, the rocks began to crack and we could move them!

Hannibal 3:　Well, this did not happen to me, but it is about me. Even years after my death, the Romans used the following phrase as a rallying cry whenever they were threatened: "Hannibal is at the gates." Of course, they said it in Latin. I understand that parents also used the phrase to frighten unruly children!

Panelist 4:　You had a very unique military idea for your attack on Rome. In addition to 60,000 troops, you brought 40 elephants across the Mediterranean Sea to Spain. You believed that since elephants had never been seen in Europe, they would frighten the people. The elephants would also act like modern tanks battering through enemy lines. Your army marched through Spain, across the Pyrenees, through France, and over the Alps into northern Italy. Many of your soldiers and "animal tanks" lost their footing on the snowy mountain passes and died. In fact, when you finally reached northern Italy, you had less than half of your army and only a few elephants left. Tell us about a memory of this military campaign.

Hannibal 1:　As we reached the Rhone River, the river was flooding and surged with rapid, flowing water. My men and I had to construct rafts to transport the elephants across the river, but they refused to budge and board the rafts. So we built ramps and covered the paths with dirt so it looked like land. Most of the elephants were fooled by the trick and boarded the rafts, but others began to charge and capsized the rafts. Many of my men drowned, but the elephants swam to safety.

Hannibal 2:　When we got to northern Italy, we needed money so I came up with a terrific idea to make some money. I told my men to set up one of our big canvas tents on the outskirts of Rome and to put the elephants inside. Several of my soldiers began roasting peanuts to sell while others went to the city to entice people to come see the unique seven-ton beasts! The elephants attracted people from everywhere who were willing to pay the 50-cent admission ticket price!

To Tell the Truth with Hannibal *(cont.)*

Hannibal 3: Going over the Alps was very dangerous because of the cold climate, which we had never experienced. The snow was very deep at some points along the mountain path. Being an athlete, I had packed two tennis rackets in my bag—a spare in case one got broken during fighting—and I ordered my men to bring tennis rackets so they could challenge me during breaks from our battles. Then I had an idea. I strapped my feet to the tennis rackets with pieces of leather from my belt and made snowshoes that allowed me to walk over the deep snow easily! My men soon followed my example.

Panelist 5: Although the Romans outnumbered you, you won a remarkable victory at Cannae in southern Italy. You arranged your soldiers in such a way that they encircled the Roman soldiers and crushed them. It is said that your army killed 50,000 Roman soldiers in one day! Yet, your victory was brief. A Roman attack on your homeland of Carthage forced you to return home to defend Carthage. Despite your efforts, Rome defeated Carthage in 201 B.C. What did you do when the war ended?

Hannibal 1: After the war, Rome allowed us to govern ourselves and I headed the government. Years later, some citizens of Carthage wanted to hand me over to the Romans to stand trial. I fled Carthage and lived in exile for many years. When it was certain that I would be captured, I remembered the promise I had made to my father to fight the Romans to my death. I then swallowed poison that I kept hidden in a ring I wore so that I would not have to surrender to my enemy.

Hannibal 2: After the war, I remembered one of the elephants I had taken on my military campaign. It had such large ears. I wrote a children's story about an elephant with ears so big that it could actually fly. My story was even turned into a movie!

Hannibal 3: My interest in elephants continued. I opened a circus that showcased dancing elephants wearing the snowshoes I invented during the war.

Host: Panelists and members of the audience, it is now time for you to decide which of our guests is the REAL Hannibal. Is it Hannibal 1, Hannibal 2, or Hannibal 3?

All right, the votes have been cast. Will the REAL Hannibal, great military leader of ancient times, please stand up?

Alexander the Great

CONNECTIONS

Literature Connection—*Alexander the Great* by Andrew Langley

This book tells the story about Alexander the Great. Born in Macedonia around 356 B.C., Alexander was a great military leader who conquered lands from Egypt to India. Alexander is famous for spreading Greek ideas to all the lands that he conquered in his short lifetime.

Content Connections—Social Studies, Ancient Cultures

This script would be a great connection to a lesson on ancient cultures of the world.

OBJECTIVE

Students will summarize and paraphrase information in texts (e.g., arrange information in sequential order; convey main ideas, critical details, and underlying meaning).

VOCABULARY

1. Introduce the key vocabulary words from the script. Write each word on the board.

2. Describe the meaning of each word and point out its use in the script.

3. Have the students locate each of the vocabulary words in the script. Ask students to use context clues to determine the meaning of each word.

4. Have students use each of the vocabulary words in a sentence that is different from the one used in the script.

   - **encourage**—to inspire with hope
   - **civilized**—to educate, to not be a savage
   - **ancestor**—a forefather, a relative from who you are descended
   - **curiosity**—eager to learn
   - **revolt**—to seek change by uprising
   - **criticize**—to find fault

BEFORE THE READER'S THEATER

1. Read the title of the script and ask the class to make predictions about the selection. What do students know about Alexander the Great? Can they think of any other famous military soldiers in history? What qualities make a good soldier?

2. Display the Idea Web graphic organizer (page 38 or ideaweb.pdf). Write *Alexander the Great* in the center. Write the following in the other three circles: *Childhood*, *Military Leader*, and *Characteristics*.

3. Read the script aloud, modeling appropriate reading strategies while you read. To help build fluency and comprehension, it is important for students to hear the script read aloud before practicing on their own.

Alexander the Great *(cont.)*

DURING THE READER'S THEATER

1. Divide the class into groups of nine to read and practice the script.

2. Students need to decide which character they will play and then highlight their parts in the script (Alexander 1–3, Host 1, and Panelists 1–5). They should also mark with a star any places where they need to pause while reading.

3. Give students a few minutes to practice reading with expression in their voices. Additionally, students may decide on a few props or materials to use during their reading. They need to use materials that can be easily acquired or assembled in the classroom.

4. After they have finished practicing, have each group perform the reader's theater for the rest of the class. You may also want them to perform for another class.

5. Ask students if they know the answer to the question "Who is the REAL Alexander the Great?" (**Note:** The REAL Alexander the Great is Alexander 2.)

6. Discuss the following questions with students:

    • Do you know of any Greek ideas that Alexander the Great spread to the cultures he conquered?

    • What are superstitions? Can you list any superstitions?

    • Have you ever watched the Olympics? What are some sports you enjoy watching?

    • What can athletes from different countries participating in the Olympics learn from one another?

AFTER THE READER'S THEATER

1. Have students complete the Idea Web graphic organizer independently or in pairs.

2. Have students research more information about Alexander the Great using books, encyclopedias, reference materials, and the Internet.

3. With this information, have students create a brochure about Alexander the Great. The brochure should have key points and information about the biography of Alexander the Great. Have students include a "Did you Know?" section in the brochure with items about Alexander the Great.

RESPONSE QUESTIONS

Group Discussion Questions

• What are some things in nature that you can observe this afternoon?

• Do you think Alexander the Great "cheated" using his method of undoing the knot? Why or why not?

Written Response Question

• Pretend you are Alexander the Great being lowered into the sea in the glass barrel. Write three things that you saw in the water and draw a picture to match.

Name _____　Date _____

Idea Web

To Tell the Truth with Alexander the Great

By Gail Skroback Hennessey

A reader's theater with nine parts

Host: Today's guest is Alexander the Great. Only one of our three guests is the REAL Alexander the Great. The other two are imposters. Your job is to listen carefully to the information presented and decide which of the three guests is the REAL Alexander the Great. Let's begin by meeting our guests.

Alexander 1: I am the great military genius of history, Alexander the Great!

Alexander 2: I am pleased to be here today. My name is Alexander the Great.

Alexander 3: Alexander the Great, that's me!

Host: Let me read this brief summary on Alexander the Great. Alexander the Great was born in 356 B.C. in Macedonia (an area that is now part of Greece, Bulgaria, and Yugoslavia). He was one of the greatest military leaders in history. By the time he was barely out of his teens, he had conquered the known civilized world. His empire included Greece and Egypt and extended as far east as India. To encourage trade with Egypt and Greece, he built a great city by the Mediterranean Sea and called it Alexandria. He also built a huge lighthouse called Pharos that was one of the great wonders of the ancient world. He was unique in the way he ruled because he granted equal rights to all citizens who became part of his empire. He was interested in learning about other cultures, so he learned the languages and customs of the people he conquered. When he was in Mesopotamia—present day Iraq—he even learned astronomy. Because he was such a curious man, he sent an expedition down the Nile River to Ethiopia to explore the region.

Yet, many people today consider Alexander to be a greedy and power-hungry villain! Regardless, he did contribute something quite important to history by spreading the progressive ideas of the Greeks to all the people he conquered. He also built museums for the many treasures he gathered on his travels and founded nearly 70 cities throughout his empire—he named most of them for himself. After 11 years of battles, Alexander never returned to Greece. His life ended suddenly at the young age of 33. Sadly, he did not die a brave soldier's death from a wound received in battle, but instead fell ill and died from a disease called malaria.

Let's begin the questioning of our three guests with Panelist 1.

To Tell the Truth with Alexander the Great *(cont.)*

Panelist 1: You were the son of King Philip of Macedonia and Queen Olympias. On the day you were born, it is said that two eagles perched on the roof of the room where you lay. Wise men at the time said this was a good sign that meant you would one day rule two great nations. Tell us, Alexander the Great, about a childhood memory.

Alexander 1: I was a very good athlete and an especially good runner. One day, someone asked if I planned to compete in the Olympic games. When I responded, "If I can have kings as my competitors," I was called conceited! Can you believe it?

Alexander 2: As a student, I learned math, writing, and reading. I also learned how to use a sword, ride horses, and throw spears. I liked music, played the harp, and enjoyed reading about famous Greek warriors.

Alexander 3: Unfortunately, my childhood was not very pleasant. My parents fought a lot. My mother told me stories about the Greek hero Achilles and said he was my ancestor. My father angrily said that she was filling my head with nonsense! At the age of 20, my father was killed at a dinner party and I became king!

Panelist 2: When you were about 13, your father hired a new tutor for you. He was the famous Greek scientist, Aristotle. From Aristotle you learned to love Greek civilization and ideals. He also taught you the importance of observing the world and people around you. Explain how you acquired the wild black colt named Bucephalus (bew-SEF-uh-lus), Greek for "bull headed," that no one was able to ride but you.

Alexander 1: When I was about 12 years old, I wanted all my father's soldiers to realize that I was the son of a king. Although Bucephalus jerked his head, snorted, kicked, and threw anyone who tried to ride him, I was determined to show my bravery and ride this horse so no one would ever call me a wimp!

Alexander 2: I noticed that the horse was really a coward. Can you believe that he was afraid of his own shadow? I simply turned the colt's head toward the sun so it could not see its shadow and mounted him bareback. My father was so impressed with me that he gave me the horse!

To Tell the Truth with Alexander the Great *(cont.)*

Panelist 3: After your father died, you became king. Some of the city-states rebelled against you because they thought you were too young and powerless to control them. You surprised the city-states by ending their revolt quickly. As an example, you burned the city of Thebes to the ground as a warning to other city-states that might think of resisting your control. Nearly 6,000 people were killed and 30,000 were sold into slavery. What do you have to say about such cruelty?

Alexander 1: Looking back, I suppose I am sorry for what I did. I guess I was having a bad day! But, happily, one of my soldiers brought along some marshmallows, so we put the fires to good use and had some tasty, toasted marshmallows.

Alexander 2: Listen, it was the custom of the time in which I lived to burn to the ground cities that revolted against the king. Besides, I did save ONE house. It belonged to the Greek poet Pindar, whose poetry I enjoyed reciting.

Alexander 3: I did not want people to think of me as a young kid. I wanted everyone to see that I was a king and in control! Besides, the buildings were old anyway and the city was in need of some remodeling!

Panelist 4: You are quoted as saying, "If my father wins any more battles, there won't be anything left for ME to conquer." You also liked Homer's *Iliad* so much that you slept with the book—along with a dagger—under your pillow each night. Tell us, Alexander the Great, do you have any other interesting experiences to share with us?

Alexander 1: Well, I will always remember when my men and I had first conquered the lands of Persia. We discovered a black liquid that would burn easily. One day, one of my men spread the black liquid on himself and someone almost accidentally set him on fire!

Alexander 3: I would sneak into the horse's barn at night and give it lots of apples. I also gave it blankets on chilly nights. After about two weeks, we were such good buddies that he let me ride him!

To Tell the Truth with Alexander the Great *(cont.)*

Alexander 2: Near Ankara, present day Turkey, was a city named Gordium. There was an old chariot with a shaft fastened to the axle by a complex knot. Nobody could untie it. Legend said that who ever could untie the knot would become king of Asia. Of course, I managed to untie the knot. No one said you had to use only your fingers to untie it, so it took just one stroke of my sword to complete the task!

Alexander 3: In 333 B.C., I climbed inside a glass barrel and one of my men put me into the Mediterranean Sea. I did this because I wanted to observe sea life. I told the people that I saw one particular fish that was so long it would take days to swim by it. NOBODY questions a king.

Panelist 5: Toward the end of your life, you began to act strangely. You believed that you were the son of the mighty Greek god Zeus and ordered people to kiss your feet. When your horse died, you gave it a large funeral and named a city in its honor. You also did the same when your favorite dog died. Any comments?

Alexander 1: I was the GREAT one. I mean, my name was Alexander the Great, was it not? As the GREAT military leader, I could do what ever I wished. Did I tell you that I also named a city for my favorite turtle? I named it "Cowabunga Dudes."

Alexander 2: Well, if you are going to criticize, you might like to know that I liked to sleep a lot and sometimes I slept the entire day. I also did not like wearing a beard, which was a custom of the time, and started a new fad of being clean-shaven.

Alexander 3: There was nothing wrong with making people kiss my feet. My feet were clean because I washed them regularly, at least once a month! Besides, I invented something I called "odor eaters," small, scented cushions you placed inside your shoes to keep them smelling nicely! These were a big hit with the people I conquered.

Host: Panelists and members of the audience, it is now time for you to decide whom you think is the REAL Alexander the Great. Is it Alexander 1, Alexander 2, or Alexander 3?

All right, the votes have been cast. Will the REAL Alexander the Great please stand up?

Leonardo da Vinci

CONNECTIONS

Literature Connection—*Leonardo da Vinci for Kids: His Life and Ideas* by Janice Herbert
This book is about Leonardo da Vinci—a scientist, inventor, and painter who was truly a remarkable man. Explore some of his most famous works, such as the *Mona Lisa* and *The Last Supper*. Students will enjoy learning about the many accomplishments and creations of this great man.

Content Connections—Art History, Science, Renaissance
This script would be a great connection to lessons about Italy, the Renaissance, art history, and science.

OBJECTIVE

Students will summarize and paraphrase information in texts (e.g., arrange information in sequential order; convey main ideas, critical details, and underlying meaning).

VOCABULARY

1. Introduce the key vocabulary words from the script. Write each word on the board.

2. Describe the meaning of each word and point out its use in the script.

3. Work with students to develop their oral language. Create a sentence frame for each vocabulary word. Write the sentence frames on the board. For example, "The apprentice has a ____ for doing great work." Show students how to complete the first sentence frame. Then ask students to complete the sentence in another way. Repeat this process with the other sentence frames.

   - **reputation**—how one is known by others
   - **impatient**—restless, unwilling to wait
   - **perfectionist**—a person who wants things to be flawless; without fault
   - **apprentice**—a beginner learning a trade
   - **dissect**—to cut apart tissue in order to exam it
   - **moat**—a ditch, usually of full of water, that surrounds a building
   - **authentic**—original or genuine

BEFORE THE READER'S THEATER

1. Read the title of the script and ask the class to make predictions about the selection. Show a picture of the Mona Lisa to students and ask them if they have heard of Leonardo da Vinci.

2. Read the script aloud, modeling appropriate reading strategies while you read. To help build fluency and comprehension, it is important for students to hear the script read aloud before practicing on their own.

Leonardo da Vinci *(cont.)*

DURING THE READER'S THEATER

1. Divide the class into groups of eight to read and practice the script.

2. Students need to decide which character they will play and then highlight their parts in the script (da Vinci 1–3, Host, and Panelists 1–4). They should also mark with a star any places where they need to pause while reading.

3. Give students a few minutes to practice reading with expression in their voices. Additionally, students may decide on a few props or materials to use during their reading. They need to use materials that can be easily acquired or assembled in the classroom.

4. After they have finished practicing, have each group perform the reader's theater for the rest of the class. You may also want them to perform for another class.

5. Ask students if they know the answer to the question "Who is the REAL Leonardo da Vinci?" (**Note:** The REAL Leonardo da Vinci is da Vinci 2.)

6. Discuss the following questions with students:

   • A good reputation is important. What three words would people use to describe you?

   • Customs are accepted behavior of a group of people. Can you think of a custom of the Chinese, Japanese, or some other group of people?

AFTER THE READER'S THEATER

1. Display the Box Summary graphic organizer (page 45 or boxsummary.pdf). Tell students that they will use the organizer to record details about Leonardo da Vinci.

2. Have students work with a partner to complete the graphic organizer.

3. If necessary, remind students to refer back to the script for more details.

RESPONSE QUESTIONS

Group Discussion Questions

• Would you like da Vinci as a friend? Give a reason why or why not.

• What are three facts you have learned about Leonardo da Vinci?

Written Response Question

• Look at a picture of Leonardo da Vinci's Last Supper and describe what you see.

Name_____ Date _____

Box Summary

To Tell the Truth with Leonardo da Vinci

By Gail Skroback Hennessey

A reader's theater with eight parts

Host: Today's guest is Leonardo da Vinci. Only one of our three guests is the REAL Leonardo da Vinci. The other two are imposters. Your job is to listen carefully to the information presented and decide which of the three guests is the REAL Leonardo da Vinci. Let's begin by meeting our guests.

da Vinci 1: Hello, my name is Leonardo da Vinci

da Vinci 2: Greetings, my name is Leonardo da Vinci.

da Vinci 3: Good day, my name is Leonardo da Vinci

Host: Let me read this brief introduction on Leonardo da Vinci. Leonardo da Vinci was born in 1452 in the village of Vinci, which is near the city of Florence in central Italy. He was one of the greatest painters of the Italian Renaissance. He painted the *Mona Lisa* and *The Last Supper*, two of the most famous paintings in the world. Although he is known to most of the world as a painter, he had many other talents. He was also an inventor, an engineer, and a sculptor. King Francis I allowed Leonardo to live at his court in France toward the end of da Vinci's life. The king said of him, "Never has any man come into this world who knew as much as da Vinci."

Host: Let's start our questioning with Panelist 1.

Panelist 1: Mr. da Vinci, what kind of a student were you?

da Vinci 1: I was an excellent student who wished to learn as much as possible about all subjects.

da Vinci 2: I was an impatient young man. I wanted to learn many things very quickly, so I rarely studied more than the introduction to the topics covered in school.

da Vinci 3: I never needed to go to school.

Panelist 2: Mr. da Vinci, tell us about what you were like as a child.

da Vinci 1: As a young child, I always tried to be neat. I always made my bed. I enjoyed having friends visit my clean and tidy room.

To Tell the Truth with Leonardo da Vinci *(cont.)*

da Vinci 2: I collected all sorts of items. I had skeletons of small animals, insects stuck on pins, snakeskin, and rocks all over my room! It was a real mess!

da Vinci 3: I did not like people to enter my room! I preferred to be alone with the sketches that littered my bedroom floor.

Panelist 3: Did you have any faults, Mr. da Vinci?

da Vinci 1: I was never very satisfied with my work. I had a bad reputation because I often did not finish the projects that I started.

da Vinci 2: I was an impatient man and a perfectionist. I always thought I could improve my work.

da Vinci 3: I was a slow worker. Sometimes this made the people who hired me angry.

Panelist 4: Mr. da Vinci, did you get any formal training in art and, if so, where?

da Vinci 1: I taught myself how to paint. I enjoyed visiting museums and I liked to trace pictures hanging on the museum walls when no one was around.

da Vinci 2: I was an apprentice for a famous painter of Florence named Verrocchio. I worked with him from about the age of 14 to 20 when I joined the painting guild!

da Vinci 3: I was an apprentice for the artist Michelangelo. He taught me a lot about painting, especially how to paint while lying on your back and how to avoid getting paint in your eyes!

Panelist 1: You liked to study the heavens and observe things around you. You dissected human and animal bodies to see the way the muscles and other organs of the body looked. You did this even though you knew that if you were caught, you would be punished by death. You believed the sun, not Earth, was the center of the universe when most people said otherwise. How did you remember what you learned, Mr. da Vinci?

da Vinci 1: I had a photographic mind, which means I always remembered what I saw!

To Tell the Truth with Leonardo da Vinci *(cont.)*

da Vinci 2: I kept a notebook. It had more than 5,000 pages. I kept a pad in my belt at all times, so I could record what I noticed. Incidentally, I wrote backwards, so no one could read over my shoulder!

da Vinci 3: Very early, I invented a device that was a great help in remembering what I observed. I called it a voice player. It was solar powered, and when I talked into the box, it recorded my voice. I could play it back whenever I wanted to hear myself.

Panelist 2: Hoping to get a job, you once wrote a letter to the Duke of Milan and said that you could "build a light and strong bridge useful in crossing moats." You also claimed that you "knew how to dig a tunnel without making noise" and that you could "make a gun and cannon which could shoot small stones like a storm." What were some of your other inventions?

da Vinci 1: I drew sketches for a flying machine.

da Vinci 2: I designed a parachute and a diving suit.

da Vinci 3: I drew sketches of an automobile that was powered by two huge springs and steered by a tiller attached to a wheel in the back.

Panelist 3: Mr. da Vinci, what is a significant memory you have?

da Vinci 1: I remember the strange looks I got when I walked into a shop, bought a bird, and then set it free outside! I loved observing flight! I wanted to fly, too. I enjoyed making paper airplanes, and I organized the first paper airplane contest ever held.

da Vinci 2: I once constructed a creature from parts of lizards, toads, bats, and snakes. I thought it was funny when I frightened my young apprentices with it!

da Vinci 3: I remember what a great person I was. I was truly a man ahead of my time.

Panelist 4: Mr. da Vinci, tell us about some of your artwork.

To Tell the Truth with Leonardo da Vinci *(cont.)*

da Vinci 1: I enjoyed painting the *Mona Lisa*. In fact, I refused to sell it to anyone after I finished it. I kept it all my life. Have you noticed that she does not have any eyebrows? That was the custom for rich women. After completing this work, I enjoyed making dots on canvas and then connecting the dots to create a figure. I thought others would really like this idea, so I sold the idea of dot-to-dot books!

da Vinci 2: *The Last Supper* is a beautiful painting I did that shows Jesus and his 12 disciples at a supper where Jesus startles them by announcing that one of the disciples will betray him. Unfortunately, I tried a new type of paint that did not stick well to the wall, and the paint began to fade within 50 years of completing this great work! The painting survives on the wall of a church in Milan, Italy. During World War II, the church was bombed, but my painting was not destroyed, so it is very sad that later people actually cut a doorway into the wall on which I had painted *The Last Supper*. Unbelievable!

da Vinci 3: Toward the end of my life I drew a self-portrait. It is the only authentic likeness of me that has been preserved. I drew it in about 1512, and it is quite a lovely work, if I do say so myself.

Host: Panelists and members of the audience, it is now time for you to decide which of our guests is the real Leonardo da Vinci. Is it da Vinci 1, da Vinci 2, or da Vinci 3?

All right, the votes have been cast. Will the REAL Mr. Leonardo da Vinci please stand up?

Louis Braille

CONNECTIONS

Literature Connection—*Out of Darkness: The Story of Louis Braille* by Russell Freedman

This informative book tells the story of a boy who lost his sight when he was only three years old. Students will enjoy learning about how one boy changed the lives of so many by bringing words to life for those who can't see.

Content Connections—Science, Inventors

This script would work nicely with a lesson on inventors or disability awareness.

OBJECTIVE

Students will summarize and paraphrase information in texts (e.g., arrange information in sequential order; convey main ideas, critical details, and underlying meaning).

VOCABULARY

1. Write the vocabulary words on the board and discuss the definitions.

2. Have the students locate each of the vocabulary words in the dictionary and discuss the meaning of each word. Call on students to use one of the vocabulary words in a sentence. This will give students practice and familiarity with using these words in a variety of ways.

3. Have the students write a letter using each of the vocabulary words in a sentence. The sentences should all be on the same topic of the letter. Discuss how these words can be used in a variety of sentences and settings.

    -   **scholarship**—financial assistance given to a student
    -   **unique**—one of a kind; different
    -   **celebrity**—a famous person
    -   **entitled**—to qualify; to be given a right to do something
    -   **opportunity**—a chance, an opening

BEFORE THE READER'S THEATER

1. Read the title of the script. Ask students questions, such as "If you lost your sight, what would you miss not seeing?" and "Have you ever seen Braille writing?"

2. Display the Main Ideas and Details graphic organizer (page 52 or mainidea.pdf). Write Louis Braille's name in the center. In the three large circles, write *Childhood*, *School*, and *Invention*. After reading the script, have children help you create a heading for the fourth circle.

3. Using the script, have students organize factual information for each heading.

4. Read the script aloud, modeling appropriate reading strategies while you read. To help build fluency and comprehension, it is important for students to hear the script read aloud before practicing on their own.

Louis Braille *(cont.)*

During the Reader's Theater

1. Divide the class into groups of seven to read and practice the script.

2. Students need to decide which character they will play and then highlight their parts in the script (Braille 1–3, Host, and Panelists 1–3). They should also mark with a star any places where they need to pause while reading.

3. Give students a few minutes to practice reading with expression in their voices. Additionally, students may decide on a few props or materials to use during their reading. They need to use materials that can be easily acquired or assembled in the classroom.

4. After they have finished practicing, have each group perform the reader's theater for the rest of the class. You may also want them to perform for another class.

5. Ask students if they know the answer to the question "Who is the REAL Louis Braille?" (**Note:** The REAL Louis Braille is Braille 2.)

6. Discuss the following questions with students:

   • What creatures use sound to help them see?

   • Why do you think other children teased Louis Braille instead of helping him?

After the Reader's Theater

1. As a class, determine the heading for the fourth circle on the graphic organizer. Then have students work with a partner to complete the organizer with facts and details from the script.

2. Have students research more information about Louis Braille using encyclopedias, reference materials, and the Internet.

3. With this information, have the students create a brochure about Louis Braille. The brochure should have key points and information about Louis Braille.

Response Questions

Group Discussion Questions

   • Why do you think Louis Braille's parents made him do chores?

   • What are three characteristics of Louis Braille that helped him accomplish his goals?

Written Response Question

   • Would you like to have lived during the early 1800s? What are three inventions you'd miss the most?

Name_____ Date _____

Main Idea and Details

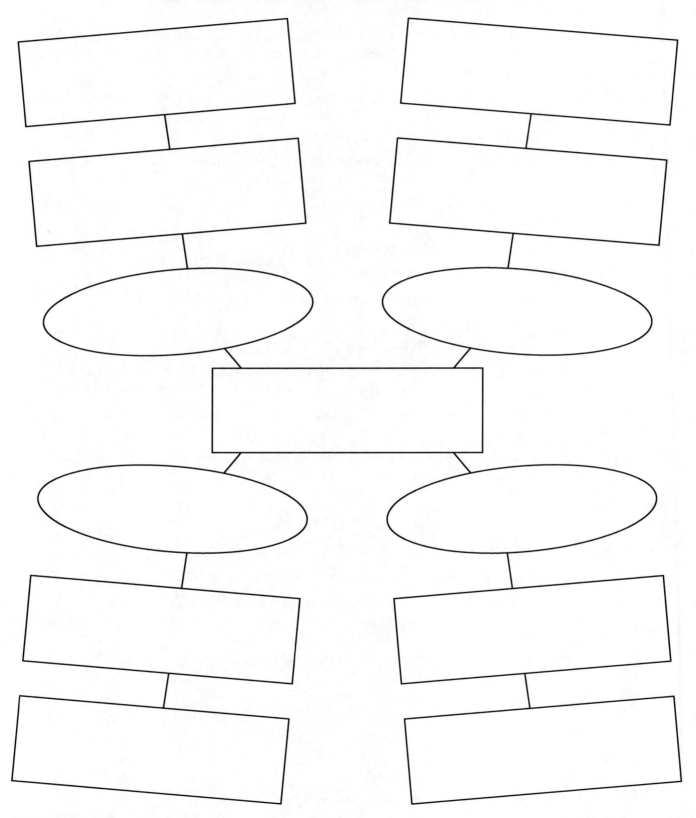

To Tell the Truth with Louis Braille

By Gail Skroback Hennessey

A reader's theater with seven parts

Host: Today's guest is Louis Braille. Only one of our three guests is the REAL Louis Braille. The other two are imposters. Your job is to listen carefully to the information presented and decide which of the three guests is the REAL Louis Braille. Let's begin by meeting our guests.

Braille 1: "Bonjour." That is French for "good day." My name is Louis Braille.

Braille 2: It is a pleasure to be here in your class today. My name is Louis Braille.

Braille 3: Hello, my name is Louis Braille.

Host: Let me read this brief summary on Louis Braille. Louis Braille was born in the village of Coupvray near Paris, France, in the year 1809. When he was about three years old, he suffered a terrible accident. He was playing in his father's harness shop with an awl—a tool used for punching holes in leather—when it slipped and pierced his eye. An infection quickly developed and spread to his other eye, leaving him totally blind. Louis wanted very much to learn, but few blind children went to school beyond the age of 10. However, Louis was lucky and was accepted to the National Institute for the Blind in Paris. At the Institute, he discovered that very few books were available for blind students. The system used to teach the blind to read required students to recognize the shapes and letters of the alphabet, which were enlarged and raised up on a page. These books were very difficult to read and expensive to produce! At the age of 11, Louis decided to develop a new system to assist the blind in learning to read and to communicate more easily. At 15, he created the writing system that uses raised dots. This system was named after him. His struggle to learn and to be treated like sighted children helped to change opinions about educating blind children. He died in 1852.

Let's begin the questioning with Panelist 1.

Panelist 1: Your parents spent many hours describing things to you, such as the town in which you lived, the countryside, and the weather. Describe some early memories of how you coped without your sight.

To Tell the Truth with Louis Braille *(cont.)*

Braille 1: Well, I often hummed or made noises as I walked. These sounds helped me "see" my way. I learned that sound waves made different sounds when they hit objects and could tell me when an obstacle blocked my way and how near it was.

Braille 2: In addition to developing my sense of hearing, I also relied on my sense of smell to recognize my surroundings.

Braille 3: Even though I was blind, my parents did not let me sit around and do nothing. They assigned me a number of chores for which I had to be responsible just like the other members of my family. I had to polish the leather, set the dinner table, and fetch buckets of water at the well.

Panelist 2: At the age of seven, you attended the village school where the teacher, Antoine Becheret, defended your enrollment in the class. Some thought that a blind boy should not be allowed to take up room on the crowded classroom benches. You worked very hard and became the top student in your class. Tell us about your early school days.

Braille 1: I remember that the girls sat on one side and the boys sat on the other side of the classroom. When it was time for the math lesson, I had to do all the problems in my head!

Braille 2: The most depressing part of the school day was reading time. I wanted to read so very much, but there were no books for blind children to read. I remember struggling not to cry during this part of the day and holding a book so I could pretend to read!

Braille 3: My sister taught me the letters of the alphabet by forming letters out of straw and making me trace over them until I learned the letters. Friends at school were also helpful and came to my house and read the lessons to me.

Panelist 3: Your hard work at the village school paid off when you received a scholarship to attend the National Institute for the Blind in Paris. You were the youngest of 60 pupils to attend this unique school. The early days at the school were difficult for you. You were away from your family for the first time and the cruel, sighted children called you names, such as "ugly eyes," and threw horse manure at you. You did not know the school and tripped over things constantly. However, eventually, you made friends and liked the school. Describe a memory of the Institute for us.

To Tell the Truth with Louis Braille *(cont.)*

Braille 1: I was very excited about the possibility of having books specially written so a blind student could read them. I spent hours every day in the library reading the many books on the shelves. I was a real bookworm!

Braille 2: Braille 1 is not correct about the books in the library. I was disappointed when I discovered that there were only 14 books in the library! When I asked why there were so few books, I was told that the process of writing a book for the blind was very expensive because only eight to ten words could be written on each page since the letters needed to be so large! With so few words on a page, a book had many pages and could weigh hundreds of pounds!

Braille 3: I remember the field trips we took so we could experience the sounds and smells of the city. We called ourselves the "rope gang," because we would walk in a line with each of us tied to a rope that was fastened to the student in front.

Panelist 1: You were only 11 when you announced that you were going to create a new way for blind people to read and communicate with others. Where did you get the idea for the Braille system that is named after you?

Braille 1: During my spare time, I enjoyed listening to my portable radio and doing dot-to-dot coloring sheets. While doing one of these fun dot-to-dot sheets, I came up with the idea of using raised dots to create a new alphabet for the blind.

Braille 3: Believe it or not, I was buttoning my shirt one morning in front of the microwave oven, which was cooking my breakfast bacon, when the idea of using raised dots to create a system that would enable the blind to read came to me.

Braille 2: A soldier named Charles Barbiers visited my school and showed me a system he used called "night writing" to communicate with his soldiers at night so they had no need to talk or use lamps that might give the army's position away to the enemy. The system involved raised dots and dashes punched on paper. I adapted this "night writing" method, using alphabet cells of six dots to create 63 possible arrangements. My system eventually included letters, numbers, punctuation, and musical signs.

Panelist 2: The Braille system you created at 15 years old enabled the blind to read books and music. You must have been a real celebrity at the Institute! Would you please tell us how the director of the Institute rewarded your efforts?

To Tell the Truth with Louis Braille *(cont.)*

Braille 1: People from all over France came to meet me and learn about my Braille system. My picture was on the cover of *Life*, *Newsweek*, and *TIME* magazines. I was even asked to travel to the United States to be a guest on the *Phil Donahue Show.*

Braille 2: The director of the Institute was so proud of me that he offered me a teaching position and granted my wish to have the school renamed the Braille Institute for the Blind.

Braille 3: Unfortunately, the other two guests are not correct about how my system was received. In fact, the school banned its use! All the works that I had translated into my dot system were burned! Many at the school felt my system would make the blind independent and secretive, because sighted people would be unable to read the system. These people did not like this possibility. Students came to my room secretly at night to learn the system even though they knew they would be punished if they were caught!

Panelist 6: Some thought your system was a trick and that no one could read by touching dots on a piece of paper. Eventually, a new director understood the importance of your system and said that blind students were entitled to learn how to be independent just like sighted students. The Institute later adopted your system. How did you spend your later years?

Braille 1: I really liked music and started a rap band that became very popular. One song that made me rich was a song I wrote to the words of the nursery rhyme, "Three Blind Mice."

Braille 3: I always liked sports and I was given the opportunity to play baseball. I joined the New York Yankees and, using a special ball that gave off a noise so I could locate it with my hearing, I became the leading catcher. I was eventually inducted into the Baseball Hall of Fame in Cooperstown, New York.

Braille 2: As Braille 1 stated, I was a very talented musician and I became the organist at St. Nicholas-des Champs, one of the largest churches in Paris. Unfortunately, I never lived to see my system gain the worldwide acceptance that it has today.

Host: Panelist and members of the audience, it is now time for you to decide which one of our guests is the REAL Louis Braille. Is it Braille 1, Braille 2, or Braille 3?

All right, the votes have been cast. Will the REAL Louis Braille please stand up?

Elizabeth Blackwell

CONNECTIONS

Literature Connection—*Elizabeth Blackwell: Girl Doctor* by Joanne Landers Henry

Born in 1849, Elizabeth Blackwell became the first woman doctor. Today, there are many women who become medical doctors, but for Blackwell, the struggle was a long and difficult one. Read this book along with the reader's theater to learn more about her accomplishment.

Content Connections—Social Studies, Women's History

This script is a great introduction for a unit on women's suffrage or during Women's History Week.

OBJECTIVE

Students will summarize and paraphrase information in texts (e.g., arrange information in sequential order; convey main ideas, critical details, and underlying meaning).

VOCABULARY

1. Introduce the key vocabulary words from the script. Write each word on the board.

2. Describe the meaning of each word and point out its use in the script. Show pictures that represent the meaning of each word if you have them.

3. Ask students to help you write a short story, using all six vocabulary words. Write the story on chart paper.

   - **persevere**—to keep trying without giving up

   - **hygiene**—cleanliness

   - **privileges**—extra rights that are an advantage or a benefit

   - **procedure**—a method used to do something

   - **perfectionist**—a person who wants everything done correctly and without mistakes

   - **implement**—to begin to use

BEFORE THE READER'S THEATER

1. Read the title of the script and ask the class to share what they know about Elizabeth Blackwell. Ask students, "Have you wanted to do something but were told you couldn't because of your age?" and "How many of you know a female doctor or go to one?"

2. Display the Cluster Web graphic organizer (page 59 or clusterweb.pdf). Write Elizabeth Blackwell's name in the center circle. In three large circles, place *Childhood*, *Becoming a doctor*, and *Dr. Blackwell*. Students need to brainstorm details from the script to add under each heading after they have read the reader's theater script.

Elizabeth Blackwell *(cont.)*

DURING THE READER'S THEATER

1. Divide the class into groups of seven to read and practice the script.

2. Students need to decide which character they will play and then highlight their parts in the script (Blackwell 1–3, Host, and Panelists 1–3). They should also mark with a star any places where they need to pause while reading.

3. Give students a few minutes to practice reading with expression in their voices. Additionally, students may decide on a few props or materials to use during their reading. They need to use materials that can be easily acquired or assembled in the classroom.

4. After they have finished practicing, have each group perform the reader's theater for the rest of the class. You may also want them to perform for another class.

5. Ask students if they know the answer to the question "Who is the REAL Elizabeth Blackwell?" (**Note:** The REAL Elizabeth Blackwell is Blackwell 2.)

6. Discuss the following questions with students:

    • What would have been the most difficult part about being Elizabeth Blackwell?

    • What do you think of a "black book"? Do your parents have rules that might put you in such a book?

    • Do you care about the "neatness" of your work as Elizabeth Blackwell did?

AFTER THE READER'S THEATER

1. Have students complete the Cluster Web graphic organizer independently or with a partner.

2. Have students research more information about Elizabeth Blackwell.

3. With this information, have students create a time line of Elizabeth Blackwell life. Distribute poster paper so students have plenty of room. Instruct students to use pictures and diagrams to illustrate their poster.

RESPONSE QUESTIONS

Group Discussion Questions

    • Why do you think Elizabeth Blackwell found success in the poor section of New York City?

    • What are some examples of good hygiene?

Written Response Question

    • Are there still jobs today that you think are still not open for women?

Name_____ Date _____

Cluster Web

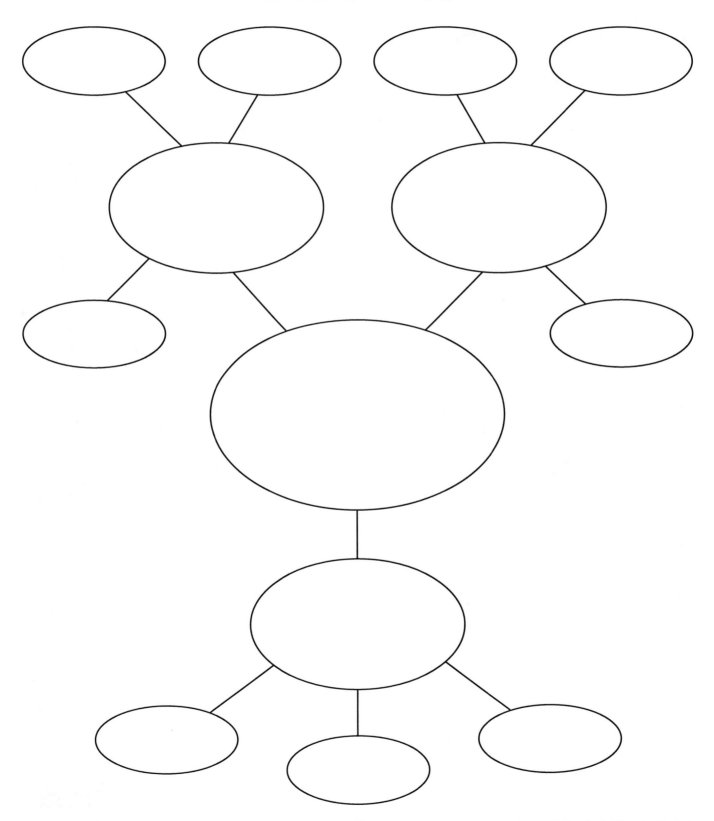

To Tell the Truth with Elizabeth Blackwell

BY GAIL SKROBACK HENNESSEY

A reader's theater with seven parts

Host: Today's Guest is Elizabeth Blackwell. Only one of our three guests is the REAL Elizabeth Blackwell. The other two are imposters. Your job is to listen carefully to the information presented and decide which of the three guests is the REAL Elizabeth Blackwell. Let's begin by meeting our guests.

Blackwell 1: I am very pleased to meet you. My name is Elizabeth Blackwell.

Blackwell 2: Good day! My name is Dr. Elizabeth Blackwell.

Blackwell 3: I am the first woman doctor, Elizabeth Blackwell.

Host: Let me read this brief summary on Elizabeth Blackwell. Elizabeth Blackwell was born in Bristol, England, in 1821. At a very young age, she decided she wanted to be a doctor. Because being a physician was not considered to be a proper job for a woman, she had great difficulty reaching her goal and encountered a great deal of prejudice. However, she persevered and eventually became the first female physician. She also established the first hospital for women in New York. Other female doctors, including her sister, ran the hospital. She wrote and published papers on the importance of hygiene in the prevention of disease. Before she died in 1910, she had lived to see an increasing number of women enter the medical profession, including her sister.

Let's begin the questioning with Panelist 1.

Panelist 1: You grew up in London where your father owned a sugar refinery. He believed in gender equality and stressed the importance of education for his sons as well as for his daughters. You learned math, geography, science, Greek, and Latin. Tell us about your childhood, Ms. Blackwell.

Blackwell 1: I was somewhat of a tomboy, and I had little interest in traditional women's activities, such as embroidery.

To Tell the Truth with Elizabeth Blackwell *(cont.)*

Blackwell 2: I grew up in a large family, and my aunt was in charge of the older children and me. If we misbehaved, she put our names in a black book that she always carried. If your name was placed in this book, you could not eat with the family or you lost all your privileges. I admit to having had my name placed in my aunt's book more times than I care to remember.

Blackwell 3: I had great ambition even at an early age. At age six, I was asked what I wanted to do when I got older, and I announced to the family that I planned to do something difficult. One family member, an aunt, said it was a pity that such a strong spirit was wasted on a girl. I did not think it was a waste!

Panelist 2: What kind of a student were you?

Blackwell 1: I did not take my schoolwork seriously. I was more interested in talking to my friends and playing outside.

Blackwell 2: I was a perfectionist. I preferred to stay inside so I could do extra work, while everyone else went outside to play! I could often be found recopying my assignments over and over so that they would look like the articles written in the textbooks!

Blackwell 3: I was very interested in science. I loved to catch frogs and study them. Climbing trees to collect leaves and bugs was another favorite pastime.

Panelist 3: Eventually your family left England and came to the United States. What made you want to become a doctor, a profession not open to women at the time?

Blackwell 1: I knew that doctors earned a lot of money and were highly respected.

Blackwell 2: When I was eight years old, I told my family that I wanted to be a doctor, but I did not think much more about the idea. One day my friend, Mary, got sick and was dying. She told me that she wished there were female doctors and that I should become a doctor. After she died, I decided to become a doctor.

Blackwell 3: I believed in equal rights for women and decided to work to change the attitudes of my time. I admit that I also I wanted the fame that being the first woman doctor would bring.

To Tell the Truth with Elizabeth Blackwell *(cont.)*

Panelist 1: No medical school would admit you, so you studied with Quaker doctors who believed in women's rights. Finally, in 1847, Geneva Medical College in New York accepted you. The officials at the college did not take you seriously at first and accepted you, in large part, as a joke. They did not think you would last more than a few weeks. Tell us about your memories of medical school.

Blackwell 1: At that time, many people believed that nice women would faint at the sight of blood. However, I did not faint and I began slowly to earn the respect of both the faculty and the students. However, at graduation, I was not placed on the list of graduates to receive a diploma!

Blackwell 2: Would you believe that most people in town refused to even speak to me because I was trying to become a doctor? It was a very lonely time for me. At the boarding house, the other women ignored me! Thankfully, the landllord befriended me.

Blackwell 3: It was not easy! No one would tell me where to purchase my books or where the classrooms were located. The faculty and the students stared at me, and I was treated rudely. Some professors refused to allow me to attend their lectures. I had to complain when I was barred from a necessary anatomy class! The situation improved after people saw that I was determined to stay and graduate!

Panelist 2: La Maternité in Paris, France was a famous school for surgery. After receiving your medical degree, you applied for admission to it. You were rejected because the school did not accept women doctors. So, even though you were a doctor with a medical degree, you attended La Maternité as a nurse so that you could learn more about anatomy and surgical techniques. You returned to the United States to open your practice. What was it like to be the first woman doctor?

Blackwell 1: I had more patients than I could handle. Everyone wanted to be treated by the celebrity woman doctor. I was called "Doctor Make-Me-Well."

To Tell the Truth with Elizabeth Blackwell *(cont.)*

Blackwell 2: It was not easy! Landlords refused to rent me space for a doctor's office, so I had to buy a house to set up my practice. I was not even allowed to hang a sign outside the house advertising that I was a doctor! People did not come to me. Women thought I should not be a doctor and men did not want to undress in front of me! However, because my practice was located in a poor section of New York City, eventually people began to come to me for help.

Blackwell 3: After all those years of schooling and fighting to become a doctor, I found that I really did not enjoy seeing patients! I turned my attention to medical research and discovered a vaccine for polio two weeks before Jonas Salk; however, he received all the credit! To make money, I marketed a sugar and honey pill, which I called "Feel Well Pills," and claimed that these pills prevented the common cold. I made a fortune.

Panelist 3: You opened a hospital for women, trained nurses, trained other women doctors, set up visiting doctor services, and wrote articles on health and medical procedures. You eventually returned to England to work for the acceptance of women doctors there. You began the National Health Society and were the first woman to be placed on the British Medical Register in 1859. Doctor, teacher, and writer: which do you feel was your most important contribution to medicine?

Blackwell 1: Being the first woman doctor was my most important contribution. And, by the way, I also got doctors interested in playing golf.

Blackwell 2: Although I am pleased that I opened doors for women in the field of medicine, I am most proud of my medical writings and contributions to medical knowledge. Many of my ideas on the importance of hygiene and education were key to preventing disease and were eventually accepted and implemented by the medical profession.

Blackwell 3: I agree with Number 2. I also feel that my work as a medical writer is my most important contribution. I was the first to say, "An apple a day keeps the doctor away," and, while in medical college, I also wrote this popular phrase: "Sticks and stones may break my bones, but names can never hurt me."

Host: Panelists and members of the audience, it is now time for you to decide which of our guests is the REAL Elizabeth Blackwell. Is it Blackwell 1, Blackwell 2, or Blackwell 3?

All right, the votes have been cast. Will the REAL Elizabeth Blackwell please stand up?

Gandhi

CONNECTIONS

Literature Connection—*Gandhi (DK Biography)* by Amy Pastan
Born in 1896, Mohandas Gandhi came to be known as the "Father of modern India." Gandhi worked to gain India's independence from Great Britain's control using nonviolent methods. Read this book along with the script to gain a deeper understanding about his life and his efforts to gain India's freedom from Great Britain.

Content Connections—Social Studies, Ancient Cultures
This script is a nice connection to a study of India. Use this script as an addition to a lesson during Black History Month or during a lesson on civil disobedience and nonviolence.

OBJECTIVE

Students will summarize and paraphrase information in texts (e.g., arrange information in sequential order; convey main ideas, critical details, and underlying meaning).

VOCABULARY

1. Introduce the key vocabulary words from the script. Write each word on the board.

2. Describe the meaning of each word and point out its use in the script.

3. Tell each student to fold a piece of paper into six squares. Brainstorm a list of possible symbols to represent each vocabulary word. Instruct students to choose six vocabulary words and then have them draw a symbol in each square and label each picture with the appropriate vocabulary word.

   - **resistance**—the act of fighting against something, or opposing
   - **partition**—a division or separation
   - **discriminate**—to not treat someone equally
   - **foreign**—from another country
   - **discourage**—to deter, to express doubt, or to dissuade
   - **majority**—the greater number; to have the most
   - **absentminded**—forgetful
   - **persevere**—to keep trying or never giving up

BEFORE THE READER'S THEATER

1. Read the title of the script and ask if the class has heard of Mohandas Gandhi. Can they tell you where India is and do they know anything about the country? What country controlled the 13 colonies and why did the colonists seek independence?

2. Read the script aloud, modeling appropriate reading strategies while you read. To help build fluency and comprehension, it is important for students to hear the script read aloud before practicing on their own.

Gandhi *(cont.)*

DURING THE READER'S THEATER

1. Divide the class into groups of seven to read and practice the script.

2. Have students work as a group to choose and highlight their parts in the script (Gandhi 1–3, Host, and Panelists 1–3).

3. Give students a few minutes to practice reading with expression in their voices. Additionally, students may decide on a few props or materials to use during their reading. They need to use materials that can be easily acquired or assembled in the classroom.

4. After practicing, each group performs the reader's theater for the class. They may also perform for another class.

5. Ask students if they know the answer to the question "Who is the REAL Gandhi?" (**Note:** The REAL Gandhi is Gandhi 3.)

6. Discuss the following questions with students:

   • Can you think of any laws in our country that were unfair and were eventually changed?

   • Why did Great Britain not try to get the Muslims and the Hindus to work together?

   • What do you know about Martin Luther King Jr.?

AFTER THE READER'S THEATER

1. Display the Sequential Order graphic organizer (page 66 or sequentialorder.pdf).

2. Have students complete the graphic organizer independently or in pairs.

3. Have students research more information about Gandhi using an encyclopedia, reference materials, and the Internet.

4. With this information, have the students write a report on their findings. Remind students to paraphrase words and not just to copy the information they find. Instruct students to include a list of the sources they used in a references cited page.

RESPONSE QUESTIONS

Group Discussion Questions

   • What are three facts that you have learned about the Hindu religion?

   • Can you think of some examples of nonviolent activities?

Written Response Question

   • Draw a picture of the Taj Mahal and write three facts that you learned about Gandhi.

Name_____   Date _____

Sequential Order

Directions: Read the first event listed below. Then pick three more events from the script to add to the graphic organizer. Remember to write the events in sequential order.

India gained independence from Great Britain
in 1947.

↓

↓

↓

To Tell the Truth with Gandhi

By Gail Skroback Hennessey

A reader's theater with seven parts

Host: Today's guest is Mohandas Gandhi. Only one of our three guests is the REAL Mr. Gandhi. The other two are imposters. Your job is to listen carefully to the information presented and decide which of the three guests is the REAL Gandhi. Let's begin by meeting our guests.

Gandhi 1: My name is Mohandas Gandhi.

Gandhi 2: I am Mohandas Gandhi.

Gandhi 3: Good day. My name is Mohandas Gandhi.

Host: Let me read this brief summary on Mohandas Gandhi. Mohandas Karamchand Gandhi was born on October 2, 1869. Many historians regard him as the father of modern India. He used methods of nonviolent resistance against the British, who controlled India, in an attempt to seek independence for his country. Others seeking change without violence, such as the American civil rights leader Martin Luther King Jr., learned from Gandhi and used his nonviolent methods as well. Gandhi urged tolerance for each other among the Muslims and Hindus of India, and he desired a united India. Unfortunately, many people did not agree with him. After India gained independence in 1947, the Muslims wanted to divide the country into India and their own country to be called Pakistan. A Hindu who disagreed with Gandhi's beliefs assassinated him in 1948.

Let's begin the questioning with Panelist 1.

Panelist 1: Mr. Gandhi, could you tell us what you were like as a child?

Gandhi 1: I was an awkward-looking child with big eyes and large ears. I did not think I was very attractive.

Gandhi 2: I was extremely shy, hated to speak in front of others, and feared the dark.

Gandhi 3: I loved to read and was not very athletic.

Panelist 2: Tell us, Mr. Gandhi, about a memory from your childhood.

To Tell the Truth with Gandhi *(cont.)*

Gandhi 1: When I was six, my cousins and I took a bronze image from a local temple. I felt so guilty about what I had done, that when we were caught, I was the only one to admit that I had done wrong.

Gandhi 2: I married at the age of 13. My parents arranged the marriage. Later on, I spoke out against this custom of child marriages.

Gandhi 3: Hindus, such as myself, believe all life is sacred and that it is wrong to kill animals for food. We do not eat meat. When I was young, a friend suggested to me that eating meat would cure my cowardice and make me strong. I tried meat a few times, but my conscience made me stop eating it.

Panelist 3: You earned a law degree in England. On your return to India, you and your wife traveled to South Africa to work. Tell us about this part of your life.

Gandhi 1: I opened a law practice and became very well known and wealthy. I used some of my money to purchase a diamond mine and opened a jewelry store, too.

Gandhi 2: I was arrested many times for refusing to obey unfair laws. I soon overcame my shyness and became a leader for the large Indian population in South Africa.

Gandhi 3: One of my first memories of South Africa was my trip on the train to Pretoria. I had purchased a first class ticket, but I was thrown off the train when I refused to move from the first class section to the "colored" section. I decided to work to defeat the racial discrimination my people faced.

Panelist 1: Under British rule, India experienced important improvements in health, transportation, and modernization. However, the British discouraged Indian customs, did not allow Indians to have a say in the government, and taxed the Indians heavily, with an especially high tax on salt. Can you recall a nonviolent activity that you organized in an effort to gain independence for India from the British?

Gandhi 1: I remember an event in Bombay, a large city in India. My supporters placed a car bomb near a British building. It exploded, killing several people, and was important in forcing the British to pay attention to our independence movement.

Gandhi 2: In Calcutta, I led 75 supporters into a factory that stored imported cloth. We were tired of having to purchase expensive foreign goods, so we burned the factory to the ground!

To Tell the Truth with Gandhi *(cont.)*

Gandhi 3: To protest high taxes on salt, I organized a 24-day march to the sea where we showed people how to make their own salt by boiling seawater. The British were very angry and many of us were arrested for this action.

Panelist 2: You stated that your name was Mohandas, yet you were often called "Mohatma." How did you get this name?

Gandhi 1: My family gave this nickname to me. You see, I was rather absentminded and was always losing my hat and asking my mother, "See my hat, ma?"

Gandhi 2: It is a name the British called me that means "troublemaker."

Gandhi 3: It is a term of affection my people gave me. It means "great soul."

Panelist 3: You once told a British leader that Britain only ruled India as long as the Indian majority was willing to let it. The British finally gave India its independence in 1947. Was this the beginning of a happy time for you?

Gandhi 1: Peace and independence in India— I had worked hard for this day.

Gandhi 2: Of course! I had worked hard for independence. I was credited with achieving it and a national holiday was created in my honor. I was famous around the world and everyone wanted my autograph, which I signed "Gandhi the Great."

Gandhi 3: Sadly, no. The Hindus and Muslims could not get along. The two groups fought and much blood was shed. I wanted a united India so when I was 78 years old, I fasted (refused to eat) until the violence ceased. I was assassinated soon afterwards.

Panelist 1: Mr. Gandhi, how do you wish to be remembered?

Gandhi 1: I would say that I want others to realize that I was the "George Washington of India"! But, I did not cut down any cherry trees!

Gandhi 2: I would like people to remember the cruel treatment the Indians suffered under British rule and that I led my people in the fight for independence.

Gandhi 3: I want to be remembered for my method of bringing about social change by nonviolent methods. Change can occur without violence if you persevere and believe in what you are doing!

Host: Panelists and members of the audience, it is now time for you to decide which of our guests is the real Gandhi. Is it Gandhi 1, Gandhi 2, or Gandhi 3?

All right, the votes have been cast. Will the REAL Gandhi please stand up?

Edgar Allan Poe

CONNECTIONS

Literature Connection—*Edgar Allan Poe's Tales of Mystery and Madness* by Edgar Allan Poe
Give a "thank you" to Edgar Allen Poe if you like detective stories. Poe is credited with writing the first true detective story requiring the reader to using thinking skills to solve the case. The American writer, born in 1809 in Boston, Massachusetts, is remembered most for his story *The Tell-Tale Heart*.

Content Connections—Language Arts, Poetry
This script is a nice connection to National Poetry Month in April or a literacy unit on famous writers.

OBJECTIVE

Students will summarize and paraphrase information in texts (e.g., arrange information in sequential order; convey main ideas, critical details, and underlying meaning).

VOCABULARY

1. Introduce the key vocabulary words from the script. Write each word on the board.

2. Describe the meaning of each word and point out its use in the script.

3. Have students work in small groups. Assign each group a vocabulary word to learn more about. Where did this word come from? How many different endings does this word have? What part of speech are these different endings?

4. Allow time for groups to share their findings with the class. Then have each group write a sentence for each word that shows the meaning of the word. Instruct groups not to use the vocabulary words in a sentence, but to use synonyms instead. For example, The author gave a *handwritten book* (manuscript) to his editor.

5. Have each group exchange their papers with another group. The group should work together to determine which vocabulary word is being described.
   - **deduct**—to figure out
   - **suspense**—a state of excitement or anticipation
   - **manuscript**—a handwritten or type-written book
   - **prank**—a trick
   - **conceited**—thinking highly of oneself; vain
   - **mischievous**—behaving in a manner that often leads to trouble
   - **hallucination**—seeing or hearing things that aren't real

BEFORE THE READER'S THEATER

1. Read the title of the script. Have students discuss what they already know about Edgar Allan Poe.

2. Display the Outline Form graphic organizer (page 72 or outlineform.pdf). Tell students that the organizer should be used to take notes about the important details found in the script.

Edgar Allan Poe (cont.)

BEFORE THE READER'S THEATER (cont.)

3. Read the script aloud, modeling appropriate reading strategies while you read. To help build fluency and comprehension, it is important for students to hear the script read aloud before practicing on their own.

DURING THE READER'S THEATER

1. Divide the class into groups of seven to read and practice the script.

2. Students need to decide which character they will play and then highlight their parts in the script (Poe 1–3, Host, and Panelists 1–3). They should also mark with a star any places where they need to pause while reading.

3. Give students a few minutes to practice reading with expression in their voices. Additionally, students may decide on a few props or materials to use during their reading. They need to use materials that can be easily acquired or assembled in the classroom.

4. After they have finished practicing, have each group perform the reader's theater for the rest of the class. You may also want them to perform for another class.

5. Ask students if they know the answer to the question "Who is the REAL Edgar Allan Poe?" (**Note:** The REAL Edgar Allan Poe is Poe 1.)

6. Discuss the following questions with students:

   • Why do you think the character in "The Tell-Tale Heart" heard the ticking of the man's heart?

   • Do you think the teacher was wrong or right to discourage Poe's writing?

AFTER THE READER'S THEATER

1. Complete the Outline Form graphic organizer as a class, or have students complete it in small groups or in pairs.

2. Have students research more information about Poe using an encyclopedia, reference materials, and the Internet.

3. Instruct the students to design a poster sharing the information they have learned about Poe. Post these posters around the school or classroom to share the information with others.

RESPONSE QUESTIONS

Group Discussion Questions

   • One of Poe's favorite books was *Robinson Crusoe*. What is your favorite book? Why?

   • What might you place on Poe's tombstone?

Written Response Question

   • Do you think you would have liked to have Poe as a friend? Why or why not?

Name_____ Date _____

Outline Form

Title: _____

I.   _____

   A.   _____

      1.   _____

      2.   _____

      3.   _____

   B.   _____

      1.   _____

      2.   _____

II.   _____

   A.   _____

      1.   _____

      2.   _____

   B.   _____

      1.   _____

      2.   _____

      3.   _____

Conclusion: _____

_____

To Tell the Truth with Edgar Allan Poe

By Gail Skroback Hennessey

A reader's theater with seven parts

Host: Today's guest is Edgar Allan Poe. Only one of our three guests is the REAL American poet and short story writer. The other two are imposters. Your job is to listen carefully to the information presented and decide which of the three guests is the REAL Edgar Allan Poe. Let's begin by meeting our guests.

Poe 1: I will say my name once, and nevermore! It's Edgar Allan Poe.

Poe 2: Hello, students! My name is Edgar Allan Poe.

Poe 3: Edgar Allan Poe, that's me. I write short stories and poetry!

Host: Let me read this brief summary on Edgar Allan Poe. Edgar Poe was born in 1809 in Boston, Massachusetts. His parents were struggling actors in a traveling theater company. His early life was very difficult. His father was an alcoholic who left the family when Edgar was a baby. His mother died from tuberculosis when he was only three. His grandfather had no interest in raising the children, so different foster families raised Edgar and his younger sister separately. Although he was never officially adopted, he eventually added Allan—the name of the family that raised him—to his name. At 23, he published his first short stories. Perhaps because he viewed his life as a sad one, his writing is often about tragic love, terror, death, and horror. One of his short stories, "The Murders in the Rue Morgue," is considered the first real detective story. Sir Arthur Conan Doyle, author of *Sherlock Holmes*, called Poe the "Father of Detective Tales" because his stories call for deductive reasoning to solve the case. Poe died when he was only 40.

Let's begin the questioning with Panelist 1.

Panelist 1: You were only three when your mother died. During your brief time with her, you and your sister lived in such poverty that you relied on others to provide food and shelter. It is reported that when she died, all you had to remember her by was a sketch she had drawn of Boston Harbor and a locket containing a strand of her hair. Tell us about the family who cared for you after your mother died.

To Tell the Truth with Edgar Allan Poe *(cont.)*

Poe 1: I was raised by a wealthy couple named Frances and John Allan. My life was quite different from what I had known before. I had my own bedroom and I even had servants to help me get ready for bed! I can remember standing in stocking feet on the dining room table. I toasted my parents' friends and recited passages of English poetry as the Allans looked on proudly.

Poe 2: Interestingly, two weeks after my mother died, the theater where she would have been performing in Richmond, Virginia, burned to the ground and 60 people, including the governor of Virginia, died. Although John Allan gave me the best of everything, he was not affectionate. He and I did not get along well. I got my share of spankings, and often had to go outside and find the switch that he used to whip me!

Poe 3: As Poe 1 stated, my life was very different after I began living with the Allans. I called them Mama and Pa, and Mama spoiled me. They gave me a pony to ride, and Mama dressed me in very fancy clothes. I remember going to one of her afternoon tea parties wearing a purple velvet cap with gold tassels, a white blouse, and baggy velvet pants!

Panelist 2: Mr. Poe, tell us about some of the stories you wrote?

Poe 1: I wrote "The Tell-Tale Heart" in the first person; that is, the main character tells the reader how and why he decides to kill the old man with whom he lives. The main character is crazy and is disturbed by the old man's eye. After he murders the man and buries him under the floor of a room, the police come to his house. The main character thinks he can hear the ticking of the dead man's heart, and fearing the police can also hear it, he confesses to the murder! It is a great suspense story!

Poe 2: Another story I wrote is "The Gold-Bug," which is about searching for Captain Kidd's buried treasure on an island. Much of the information for this story I learned on nature walks with a biologist who taught at my school in England.

To Tell the Truth with Edgar Allan Poe *(cont.)*

Poe 3: The poem "The Raven" made me famous overnight. The poem is about lost love and grief. The raven says only one word, "Nevermore," but he repeats it over and over, emphasizing a lover's grief over a love that will "nevermore" be. Another of my famous stories is called "The Fall of the House of Usher" and is about a twin brother and sister who are very close. After the sister dies, the brother continues to hear noises and begins to believe that he has mistakenly buried her while she was still very much alive!

Panelist 3: Your "adopted" parents sent you to the best private schools and even took you to live in England for a time. You lived a very comfortable life. What kind of student were you, Mr. Poe?

Poe 1: I was very athletic, and although I was once described as "thin as a razor," I developed a muscular body from my physical activities. I was especially good at the broad jump and swimming. I was also quite musical and very intelligent.

Poe 2: I was a daydreamer who rarely listened in class and turned on my portable music player to listen to music whenever I could. Unfortunately, one day my teacher caught me and took one of my favorite Elvis Presley tapes!

Poe 3: I was a hard worker and good at learning languages, such as French and Latin. Because I was athletic, I was very popular. Like my real mother, I also loved to draw and I covered the walls of my room with crayon sketches of the countryside!

Panelist 1: You were interested in writing at an early age. At the age of 11, you showed a manuscript of some poems to your schoolteacher hoping that he could get them published. Although the teacher liked your work, he felt that such early success would make you conceited, so he discouraged your writing. I suppose you never did anything mischievous when you were a boy?

Poe 1: Well, actually, I did. I enjoyed playing pranks. My favorite prank was snatching a chair away from someone who was about to sit down. My school sent misbehaving students home with a necklace of vegetables hung around their necks. I remember that I was sent home in this manner.

Poe 2: Since I knew that John Allan would punish me severely for anything I did wrong, I learned very early to behave.

To Tell the Truth with Edgar Allan Poe *(cont.)*

Poe 3: I did not participate in mischievous activities. I was a serious student who, when not studying, was busily typing the ideas that had popped into my head during the day on my computer. However, I must admit that at times I did play computer games. I was not all work and no play!

Panelist 2: When you and the Allans returned from England, you spent the 36-day voyage learning about sea life and listening to stories of hurricanes and mutinies from the crew. You later wrote about these things. What else influenced your writing?

Poe 1: Many of my later stories reflect my own experiences. An early influence was the author Daniel Defoe. I especially liked his book *Robinson Crusoe*. It was one of my first pleasant memories of reading. I liked the way Defoe used his imagination within realistic settings. I think this affected my writing style.

Poe 2: A big influence on my later stories was a television show I loved to watch called "The Twilight Zone." The stories were real scary and I huddled in fright each Friday night in front of the television, watching each episode while munching on nacho-flavored popcorn!

Poe 3: If I had not become a writer, I would have been a doctor, specifically, a cardiologist. When I was about 15, I was flipping the dial on the satellite disk that the Allans had recently purchased and I discovered a televised operation of a heart transplant. Seeing that heart beating outside the body was awesome! I jotted down some notes and eventually wrote "The Tell-Tale Heart"!

Panelist 3: You argued often with John Allan. He felt that you were spoiled and ungrateful for all he had done for you. When you were at the University of Virginia, he did not send you enough money to live, so you started gambling to raise money to purchase books and clothing. The gambling forced you into debt and you had to leave the university. You left the Allans at the age of 18 and enlisted in the army. After your discharge, you entered the West Point Military Academy, but soon decided you did not want a military career. Your life was very hard from then on. Since you did not make enough money from your writing to live—you once wrote you were so poor that you could not afford a postage stamp—you worked as an editor and a literary critic. Your perfectionism made you very critical of other writers' work, and your criticisms angered many of them. You eventually became famous with the publication of your poem "The Raven" in 1845 and then many publishers wanted to publish your other work. Your life seemed to be taking a turn for the better. Did your fame and fortune continue?

To Tell the Truth with Edgar Allan Poe *(cont.)*

Poe 1: Unfortunately, this was not the case. Despite my success as a writer, most of the time, I barely had enough money to live. Usually, I was responsible and hard working, but I had a drinking problem and, eventually, it made it hard for me to keep a job. Also, my wife suffered from tuberculosis, the same illness that killed my mother, and died two years after the publication of "The Raven." After her death, I was very sad and continued to drink. Some say that my story ideas resulted from hallucinations that I may have had while drinking. I was found unconscious on the streets of Baltimore in 1849 and died a few days later.

Poe 2: After the success of "The Raven," I hosted my own weekly radio show where I read my poetry, especially poems about lost loves, such as Lenore and Annabel Lee. I even asked viewers to call into the show and ask my advice on their love lives.

Poe 3: I did not like being poor, especially after growing up with the wealthy Allans. Once I became famous and had money, I decided to invest it to earn more money so I could spend all my time writing. A man asked me to invest in his idea to open a place where people could buy hamburgers, French fries, sodas and milk shakes. He wanted to call it McDonald's. I thought it was a great idea; we made millions together!

Panelist 7: You once said that you disliked the dark and rarely went out at night. What else are you famous for saying?

Poe 1: I once said, "To dream has been the business of my life."

Poe 2: "Many's the long night I've dreamed of cheese toasted, mostly."

Poe 3: I am very famous for saying, "We hold these truths to be self-evident; that all men are created equal."

Host: Panelists and members of the audience, it is time to decide which of our guests is the REAL Edgar Allan Poe. Is it Poe 1, Poe 2, or Poe 3?

All right, the votes have been cast. Will the REAL Edgar Allan Poe please stand up?

Harriet Tubman

CONNECTIONS

Literature Connection—*Who Was Harriet Tubman?* by Yona Zeldis McDonough

Harriet Tubman was born of slave parents around 1820. After running away to the North and gaining her freedom from slavery, Tubman went on to help about 300 other slaves escape to freedom. Additionally, Tubman went on to work as a spy and nurse for the Union Army during the Civil War and worked to help women gain the right to vote.

Content Connections—Social Studies, Women's History, Black History

This script is a nice connection to both Women's History Month and Black History Month.

OBJECTIVE

Students will use reading skills and strategies to understand a variety of informational texts (e.g., textbooks; biographical sketches; essays).

VOCABULARY

1. Introduce the key vocabulary words from the script. Write each word on the board.

2. Describe the meaning of each word and point out its use in the script. Show pictures that represent the meaning of each word if you have them.

3. Help students deepen their understanding of the vocabulary words by creating charts of related words and pictures. For the word *disguise*, examples of disguises might include costume, mask, hide, or pretend. Post these charts in the room for students to refer to throughout the lesson.

   - **plantation**—a large farm
   - **potion**—a drink of medicine or poison
   - **disguise**—to change one's appearance
   - **fracture**—to break or crack
   - **extend**—to reach out or stretch
   - **conductor**—a leader or guide

BEFORE THE READER'S THEATER

1. Read the title of the script and ask the class what they know about Harriet Tubman. What was the Underground Railroad? Show a map of the United States and have students name the states that allowed slavery and discuss the Civil War.

2. Display the Attributes Diagram graphic organizer (page 80 or attributesdiagram.pdf). Tell students that the organizer is used to record details about a particular person.

Harriet Tubman *(cont.)*

BEFORE THE READER'S THEATER *(cont.)*

3. Read the script aloud, modeling appropriate reading strategies while you read. To help build fluency and comprehension, it is important for students to hear the script read aloud before practicing on their own.

DURING THE READER'S THEATER

1. Divide the class into groups of 10 to read and practice the script.

2. Students need to decide which character they will play and then highlight their parts in the script (Tubman 1–3, Host, and Panelists 1–6). They should also mark with a star any places where they need to pause while reading.

3. Give students a few minutes to practice reading with expression in their voices. Additionally, students may decide on a few props or materials to use during their reading. They need to use materials that can be easily acquired or assembled in the classroom.

4. After they have finished practicing, have each group perform the reader's theater for the rest of the class. You may also want them to perform for another class.

5. Ask students if they know the answer to the question "Who is the REAL Harriet Tubman?" (**Note:** The REAL Harriet Tubman is Tubman 1.)

6. Discuss the following questions with students:

   • Could you have hidden in a manure pile if it meant escaping to freedom?

   • What actions by Tubman might have frightened you if you were part of her group of slaves?

   • Why do you think Harriet's husband, John, decided not to go with her? Could you have left your loved ones to get your freedom?

AFTER THE READER'S THEATER

1. Demonstrate how to use the Attributes Diagram graphic organizer by writing Harriet Tubman in the center circle. Then write the following attributes in the circles: *courageous*, *determined*, *loyal*, and *adventurous*.

2. Have students work with a partner to find examples from the script to support each attribute. Instruct them to write their responses on the lines under the circles.

RESPONSE QUESTIONS

Group Discussion Questions

   • Find two examples of how Harriet showed "cunning" in her escape efforts.

   • Harriet used nature to help her go north. Do you know any other ways to predict things?

Written Response Question

   • Write a diary entry of someone that was on one of Tubman's escape runs and include three specific facts learned from the script.

Name_____ Date _____

Attribute Diagram

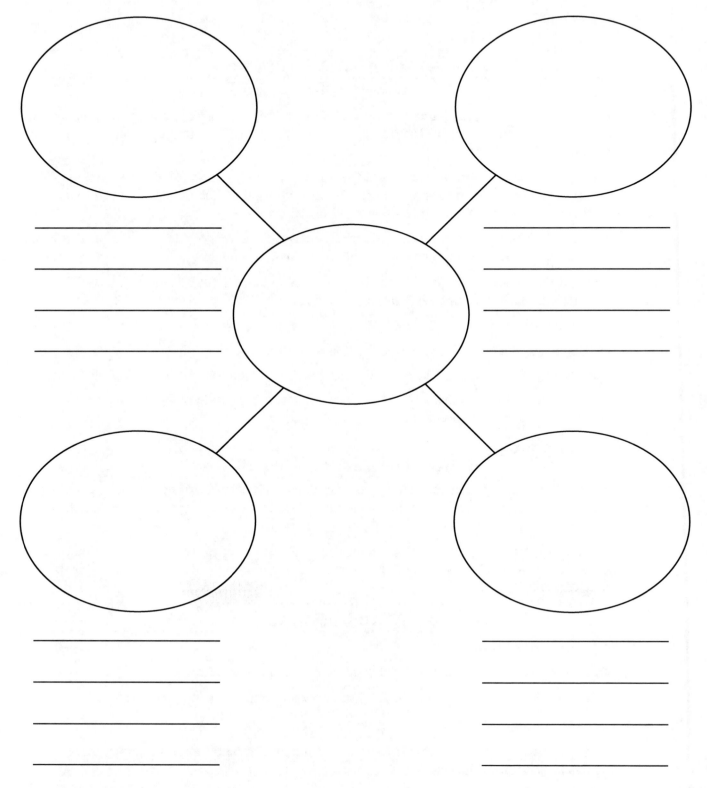

To Tell the Truth with Harriet Tubman
By Gail Skroback Hennessey
A reader's theater with ten parts

Host: Today's guest is Harriet Tubman. Only one of our three guests is the REAL Harriet Tubman. The other two are imposters. Your job is to listen carefully to the information presented and decide which of the three guests is the REAL Harriet Tubman. Let's begin by meeting our guests.

Tubman 1: Good day. I was born Araminta Ross, but I am better known by the name Harriet Tubman.

Tubman 2: It is my pleasure to be with you today. My name is Harriet Tubman.

Tubman 3: The people I led to freedom called me "Moses," but you can call me Harriet Tubman.

Host: Let me read this brief summary on Harriet Tubman. Harriet Tubman was born around the year 1820. Because no one officially recorded her birth and few slaves could read or write, her exact birth date is not known. Her parents were slaves on the plantation of a Maryland planter named Edward Brodas. When she was about 28, she learned that Brodas planned to sell her. A Quaker woman helped her escape to Philadelphia on what was called the Underground Railroad, which was not really a railroad but rather a system of cooperation by people who helped slaves escape to freedom. Once free, Harriet decided to return to the South and help other slaves escape, including most of her family. Between 1850 and 1860, she made 19 trips to the South and helped more than 300 slaves to freedom along the Underground Railroad. At one point, authorities offered a $40,000 reward for her capture, and that was a fortune in those days! During the Civil War, she was a spy and a nurse for the Union army. Later, she worked to help women earn the right to vote and opened a home for sick and elderly African Americans. During the years that she helped slaves escape to freedom, she never lost a passenger!

Let's begin the questioning with Panelist 1.

To Tell the Truth with Harriet Tubman *(cont.)*

Panelist 1: During your many trips to bring slaves to freedom, you had to worry about slave catchers and their nasty dogs hunting you down. You and your group of escapees would hide in abandoned sheds, drainage ditches, tobacco barns, and potato holes (places where farmers stored their winter vegetables). You even hid in a manure pile one time and breathed through straws until it was safe to continue your journey. Ms. Tubman, tell us about one of these journeys to freedom.

Tubman 1: One time, slave catchers were right behind me, so I decided to sit down, calmly hold a book and pretend to read. Since I could not actually read, I prayed that I was holding the book correctly! As the slave catchers walked by, I heard one of them say, "She can't be the woman we're looking for because Tubman can't read."

Tubman 2: One time, I stole a slave owner's buggy and my passengers and I rode right by some slave catchers. No one suspected us because it looked like we were on an errand for the owner of the plantation. Besides, no runaway slaves would think to escape with their owner's buggy, would they?

Tubman 3: I often wore disguises, especially after the reward posters appeared. One time, I dressed as an old woman and walked down the street with two hens tied around my waist. A plantation owner who once owned me walked right toward me! Fearing he would recognize me, I realized that I could not run away without causing more suspicion. So, I had an idea. I freed the hens and began hollering, pretending to run after them. I was actually running to safety before the man could recognize me!

Panelist 2: As a young girl, a supervisor mistakenly hit you in the head with a scale weight he meant to throw at another slave who had tried to run away. The accident fractured your skull and you almost died. For the rest of your life, you experienced blackouts that caused you to fall asleep for extended periods of time. These blackouts occurred suddenly and without warning. Your blackouts must have frightened those you were taking north to freedom. Tell us, Ms. Tubman, what was it like on your trips to freedom.

To Tell the Truth with Harriet Tubman *(cont.)*

Tubman 1: I am sure that my blackouts did frighten members of my group, but they knew to hide quietly in the bushes until I woke up. I also had a pistol and was not afraid to use it should a member of my group get scared and try to turn back! I told them, "Live north or die!" You see, any runaway who returned was beaten until he or she told how they had escaped and who had helped them. I could not allow this to happen because it would expose the Underground Railroad.

Tubman 2: The largest group I ever took to freedom at one time was 25 escaped slaves. We were constantly afraid and babies especially were a threat to our safety should they begin to cry. I always carried a medicine that would put the babies to sleep until we reached safety.

Tubman 3: I am sure that sometimes the people in my group thought my actions were strange. Sometimes, we headed further south in order to get away, because I knew the slave catchers on our trail would never think that we would go in that direction.

Panelist 3: It is said that since you were unable to read, you once slept on a park bench unaware that a nearby poster offered a reward for your capture. How were you able to find your way north, not just once, but 19 times if you could not read?

Tubman 1: My daddy once told me to follow the direction of the North Star and that is what I did. Sometimes, when the sky was cloudy, I felt tree trunks, searching for the moss because my daddy had told me that moss always grows on the north side of a tree. This tip also guided me north!

Tubman 2: To find my way north, I used a compass that I had purchased at the local general store prior to my first escape north. I also bought a pair of purple-colored sunglasses and a sunbonnet to disguise myself.

Tubman 3: I did not really need to know which direction was north. All I had to do was get to the Underground Railroad station and hop on a train to take me north. Unfortunately, there was no dining car and I got rather hungry on the long trip!

Panelist 4: When you were about 24 years old, you married John Tubman, a free black man who lived near the Brodas plantation. Being married to a free black man did not change your slave status and when you heard you were to be sold "down south," you decided to run for freedom. Tell us, Ms. Tubman, about you and your husband.

To Tell the Truth with Harriet Tubman *(cont.)*

Tubman 1: Sadly, John did not want to go north with me. In fact, he threatened to tell if I tried to run away! So, I left one night when he was asleep. Years later, when I returned to the area to help him escape, I found that he had remarried and had forgotten me! I still cared for him and that's why I continued to use the name Tubman.

Tubman 2: My husband John and I were very much in love. My husband stayed by my side through out my life and became an active member of the Underground Railroad.

Tubman 3: John Tubman and I escaped to the North where he enjoyed the colder climate and especially the snow. When I was away on trips to rescue slaves from the South, John ran the family business, a ski shop.

Panelist 5: You usually started your group's escape from a plantation on a Saturday night. You chose Saturday night because no newspapers were published on Sundays, and, therefore, no announcements about escaped slaves would be published until Monday. Search parties could not get organized until Monday, giving you and your group a head start between you and the slave catchers. How did you get word to slaves that you were in the area and willing to help them escape?

Tubman 1: Well, I loved to sing and would signal that I had come to help by singing, "Oh, go down, Moses, way down into Egypt's land. Tell old Pharaoh, let my people go." This could be why I got the nickname "Moses," because I helped my people to freedom like Moses helped his people in the Bible.

Tubman 2: I put up posters of a man sitting in a bathtub. My "Tub Man" signs let everyone know that I was in the area. Kind of clever, don't you think?

Tubman 3: I used the telephone and called all the slaves in the area and asked them if they would like to escape. Because of my telephone calls to slaves hoping to escape, the telephone company used my idea, "Reach out and touch someone," in their advertisements.

Panelist 6: During the Civil War, you served as a nurse and a spy. You were involved in one particular raid on South Carolina's Combahee River and helped free 750 slaves. What was your life like after the Civil War?

To Tell the Truth with Harriet Tubman *(cont.)*

Tubman 1:   After the war, I learned that although African Americans were free, we were not going to be treated like white people. One day, I boarded a train and the conductor told me to get out of the car. He said that African Americans could only ride in the baggage car. When I said that I was free and had every right to sit in the passenger car, I was pulled from my seat and thrown into the baggage car. I had gone through the Civil War without getting a scratch, but I got bruises when I tried to ride a train car with white people!

Tubman 2:   John wrote a best-selling book about my adventures and we were both frequent guests on television talk shows. We lived happily ever after and we were quite wealthy.

Tubman 3:   After the war, I purchased a van and traveled across the United States giving speeches about my activities during the Civil War and as a conductor for the Underground Railroad. I eventually recorded a music video that was really popular and made me a fortune!

Host: Panelists and members of the audience, it is time for you to decide which guest is the REAL Harriet Tubman. Is it Tubman 1, Tubman 2, or Tubman 3?

All right, the votes have been cast. Will the REAL Harriet Tubman please stand up?

Emily Dickinson

CONNECTIONS

Literature Connection—*Poems for Youth* by Emily Dickinson
Born in Amherst, Massachusetts, in 1830, Emily Dickinson is considered one of the best female poets. She wrote more than 1,700 poems. Her desire for privacy—rarely leaving her house—made her a woman of mystery.

Content Connections—Language Arts, Poetry
This script is a nice connection to both Women's History Month and National Poetry Month.

OBJECTIVE

Students will use reading skills and strategies to understand a variety of informational texts (e.g., textbooks; biographical sketches; essays).

VOCABULARY

1. Introduce the key vocabulary words from the script. Write each word on the board.

2. Describe the meaning of each word and point out its use in the script. Show pictures that represent the meaning of each word if you have them.

3. Ask students to help you write a short story, using all six vocabulary words. Write the story on chart paper.
   - **solitude**—being alone
   - **recluse**—someone who lives in isolation
   - **stroll**—to walk in a leisurely way
   - **glimpse**—a quick look
   - **independent**—self-reliant, doing something without help or guidance from others
   - **anonymous**—nameless; unknown

BEFORE THE READER'S THEATER

1. Read the title of the script and ask students if they have ever heard of Emily Dickinson. Have they ever written a haiku or other type of poem? Do they like reading poetry?

2. Display the Compare and Contrast graphic organizer (page 88 or compareandcontrast.pdf). Tell students they will use this organizer to record information about Harriet Tubman and Emily Dickinson. Brainstorm a few ways they are similar and different. For example, they were both determined; Tubman was outspoken but Dickinson was quiet and private.

3. Read the script aloud, modeling appropriate reading strategies while you read. To help build fluency and comprehension, it is important for students to hear the script read aloud before practicing on their own.

Emily Dickinson *(cont.)*

DURING THE READER'S THEATER

1. Divide the class into groups of nine to read and practice the script.

2. Students need to decide which character they will play and then highlight their parts in the script (Dickinson 1–3, Host, Panelists 1–5). They should also mark with a star any places where they need to pause while reading.

3. Give students a few minutes to practice reading with expression in their voices. Additionally, students may decide on a few props or materials to use during their reading. They need to use materials that can be easily acquired or assembled in the classroom.

4. After they have finished practicing, have each group perform the reader's theater for the rest of the class. You may also want them to perform for another class.

5. Ask students if they know the answer to the question "Who is the REAL Emily Dickinson?" (**Note:** The REAL Emily Dickinson is Dickinson 3.)

6. Discuss the following questions with students:

    *   Have you ever stood out from the group by doing something different? How did you feel?

    *   If you were only to wear one color, which color would you wear and why?

    *   Have you ever needed to write something down and not had any paper? What did you do?

AFTER THE READER'S THEATER

1. Have students complete the Compare and Contrast graphic organizer independently, with a partner, or in small groups.

2. Have students research more information about Emily Dickinson using an encyclopedia, reference materials, and the Internet.

3. With this information, have the students write a report on their findings. Remind students to paraphrase words and not just to copy the information they find. Instruct the students to list the sources they used in a references cited page.

RESPONSE QUESTIONS

Group Discussion Questions

*   Give three characteristics of Emily's sister, Lavinia.

*   Why do you think Emily didn't wish to publish her poems?

*   Would you have liked Emily Dickinson for a friend? Give two reasons why or why not.

Written Response Question

*   It's been a mystery as to why Emily Dickinson became a recluse. Write a reason for why Emily didn't leave the house or write a letter to Emily trying to convince her why she should leave her home.

Name_____ Date _____

Compare and Contrast

How are these two alike?

_____

_____

_____

How are these two different?

_____	_____
_____	_____
_____	_____
_____	_____
_____	_____
_____	_____
_____	_____
_____	_____

To Tell the Truth with Emily Dickinson

BY GAIL SKROBACK HENNESSEY

A reader's theater with nine parts

Host: Today's guest is Emily Dickinson. Only one of our three impersonators is the REAL American poet. The other two are imposters. Your job is to listen carefully to the information presented and decide which of the three guests is the REAL Emily Dickinson. Let's begin by meeting our guests.

Dickinson 1: Good Day to all of you! It is a pleasure to be with you today. My name is Emily Dickinson.

Dickinson 2: Emily Dickinson is my name and telling about my poetry is why I came!

Dickinson 3: Greetings, everyone. My name is Emily Dickinson.

Host: Let me read this brief summary on Emily Dickinson. Emily Dickinson was born in Amherst, Massachusetts, in 1830. As a child, she discovered the wonder of words. She once said, "A word is dead, when it is said, some said. I say it just begins to live, that day." As a girl, she liked to write humorous stories for school and would spend many late nights writing poetry after everyone else had gone to sleep. As Emily grew older, she became a very private person who rarely left her house and seldom received visitors. She liked her solitude, and many of her friendships were conducted through letter correspondence. She once said, "I don't cross my father's ground to any house or town." Some called her mysterious. Others said she was "half cracked." Some people actually strolled by her house just to catch a glimpse of her! She wrote more than 1,700 poems and most were discovered after her death by her sister. Her poems deal with fear, death, love, God, friendship, and the world. Her poems were not published until after her death at 56. She has been called America's greatest female poet.

Let's begin the questioning with Panelist 1.

To Tell the Truth with Emily Dickinson *(cont.)*

Panelist 1: As a child you were adventuresome and loved the outdoors. Your father was very strict and said that reading for pleasure was a waste of time and you should only read the Bible during your "free time." One of his house rules demanded that everyone rise early in the morning. One night your father found you writing in your bedroom in the early morning hours. He asked what you were doing and you told him that you were writing poetry. He asked to hear one of your poems, and after hearing it, canceled the early morning rising rule for you. What are some other memories of your childhood, Ms. Dickinson?

Dickinson 1: I remember how much I enjoyed studying the dictionary, especially *Webster's Unabridged Dictionary* (1847). I took it everywhere I went and liked to find new words—words to experiment with and to play with!

Dickinson 2: As a girl, I remember a book by Charles Dickens that I really enjoyed reading. Since I knew my father would not approve, I hid it outside behind a bush or underneath the piano cover so my father would not see it!

Dickinson 3: Two books that I especially enjoyed were *Wuthering Heights* by Emily Bronte and *Jane Eyre* by Charlotte Bronte. I really enjoyed the way these two authors used words to make a story come alive!

Panelist 2: You enjoyed learning and especially liked botany (the study of plants and flowers). You also enjoyed reading the plays of William Shakespeare. At 17, you were accepted at Mount Holyoke Female Seminary. Tell us about your schooling at this institution.

Dickinson 1: While at Mount Holyoke Female Seminary, I joined the ski club, the computer club, and the poetry club. I made lots of friends and was quite popular.

Dickinson 2: One memory I have about my schooling was the day I entered and won a poetry contest. I learned about Neil Armstrong's historic walk on the moon in science class and decided to write a poem about what it must have been like to see the moon first hand. It was called "Is the Moon Really Made of Cheese?" After winning the poetry contest, I was interviewed on the television program *60 Minutes*. People wanted to hear more of my poems. It was quite an exciting time in my life!

To Tell the Truth with Emily Dickinson *(cont.)*

Dickinson 3: I believed one should always tell the truth and never lie. The head of the school expected all students to publicly stand and show their faith in becoming a Christian. Since I did not feel that I could do this, I refused to stand. I was the only girl in the school who did not rise. Later, when we were told to stay in our rooms and meditate, I chose to walk outside and enjoy the beauty of the day instead. I decided early on in life to be an independent thinker!

Panelist 3: As you grew older, you became a recluse, which means you rarely left your home. You wore only white, and if people called at your home, you ran and hid until they left. In fact, it is said, that you eventually had your sister address all your many letters because you did not want your handwriting exposed to the public. Can you explain your behavior?

Dickinson 1: I guess I stayed at home because I really did not need anything outside of my home. My friends and I corresponded through letters. My house had a beautiful garden where I spent time when I was not writing poetry. Besides, I had a great sister who ran all of my errands for me!

Dickinson 2: I stayed at home because I often had bad hair days and did not want anyone to see how awful I looked. Also, my face often broke out because I loved chocolate and potato chips and I did not want anyone to see me. I guess I was overly self-conscious of my looks!

Dickinson 3: My behavior remains a mystery to many who have studied my life because I never told anyone why I chose a world of solitude. Some say that for me to write truly about the world that I needed to seclude myself because I could see the world more clearly from a distance.

Panelist 4: You wrote your poetry ideas on whatever paper was nearby and often wrote thoughts on the backs of recipes, the insides of envelopes, and on the backs of grocery lists. You often carried a pencil, so that if a word or idea occurred to you, you could jot it down immediately. After you died, your sister found unfinished poems of yours in various stages of writing. You even revised and edited your many letters again and again until you got them just right. Tell us about how you wrote.

To Tell the Truth with Emily Dickinson *(cont.)*

Dickinson 1: I used colored, scented markers and especially found that writing with a grape scent seemed to give me an extra creative flair.

Dickinson 2: Eventually, my sister, Lavinia, purchased a computer for me. I guess she was tired of picking up the scraps of paper with my writing ideas and placing them in my writing basket. With a computer, I could quickly type my thoughts, but sometimes I forgot to plug in the power pack before going to sleep.

Dickinson 3: I wrote most of my poetry and letters in pencil rather than ink. An ink pen had to be continuously dipped into ink after every few words and this made writing too slow for me. Also, pens were much more expensive than pencils.

Panelist 5: In 1862, you sent several of your poems to the editor of the *Atlantic Monthly*. You asked him to advise you on your work. He did not think that your work was publishable, but you continued to correspond with him for many years. It is said that although you sought his suggestions about your poetry, you did not listen to his advice. Another important person in your life was your friend, Helen Hunt Jackson. She loved your poetry and had several of your poems published anonymously, since she knew you would not approve. Please share one of your poems with us.

Dickinson 1: I once said, " My fellow Americans, ask not what your country can do for you. Ask what you can do for your country." Sounds great, if I do say so myself.

Dickinson 2: I once made up a children's jump rope song with words for each letter of the alphabet. Let me give you an example. "A, my name is Alice and my husband's name is Al and we come from Alabama and we sell Apples."

Dickinson 3: I once said, "If I can stop one heart from breaking, I shall not live in vain. If I can ease one life from aching or cool one pain or help one fainting robin into its nest again, I shall not live in vain."

Host: Panelists and members of the audience, it is time for you to decide whom you think is the real Emily Dickinson. Is it Dickinson 1, Dickinson 2, or Dickinson 3?

All right, the votes have been cast. Will the REAL Emily Dickinson please stand up?

Mark Twain

CONNECTIONS

Literature Connection—*Mark Twain for Kids: His Life and Times* by Kent B. Rasmussen

Tom Sawyer, *The Adventures of Huckleberry Fin*, and *A Connecticut Yankee in King Arthur's Court* are just a few of the works of this famous writer. Born in 1835, Samuel Clemens grew up to be one of the greatest humorists in American literature better known under his writing name of Mark Twain.

Content Connection—Social Studies, American Writers

This script is a nice connection to lessons about famous writers.

OBJECTIVE

Students will use reading skills and strategies to understand a variety of informational texts (e.g., textbooks; biographical sketches; essays).

VOCABULARY

1. Introduce the key vocabulary words from the script. Write each word on the board.

2. Describe the meaning of each word and point out its use in the script.

3. Have students work with a partner to list all the endings that each vocabulary word can have. For example, some of the common endings are *-ing*, *-ed*, *-er*, *-es*, and *-s*. Do these endings change the meaning of the word?

4. Instruct students to write a sentence for each of the vocabulary words using a different ending. For example, students can write a sentence for *instills* instead of *instill*.

   - **drawl**—a type of speech with drawn out vowels
   - **concentrate**—to focus your attention
   - **exaggerate**—to stretch the truth or overstate
   - **privilege**—a special right
   - **instill**—to cause one to put a feeling into practice
   - **dictate**—to speak or read aloud for another person to record

BEFORE THE READER'S THEATER

1. Read the title of the script and ask students if they know about Mark Twain. What type of information do they think they will learn about him? Do they know any facts about the Mississippi River?

2. Display the Question Strips graphic organizer (page 95 or questionstrips.pdf). Tell students that they will use the organizer to record questions they have about Mark Twain.

3. Read the script aloud, modeling appropriate reading strategies while you read. To help build fluency and comprehension, it is important for students to hear the script read aloud before practicing on their own.

Mark Twain (cont.)

DURING THE READER'S THEATER

1. Divide the class into groups of seven to read and practice the script.

2. Students need to decide which character they will play and then highlight their parts in the script (Twain 1–3, Host, and Panelists 1–3). They should also mark with a star any places where they need to pause while reading.

3. Give students a few minutes to practice reading with expression in their voices. Additionally, students may decide on a few props or materials to use during their reading. They need to use materials that can be easily acquired or assembled in the classroom.

4. After they have finished practicing, have each group perform the reader's theater for the rest of the class. You may also want them to perform for another class.

5. Ask students if they know the answer to the question "Who is the REAL Mark Twain?" (**Note:** The REAL Mark Twain is Twain 3.)

6. Discuss the following questions with students:

   • Did you ever throw rocks into a river or lake? What thoughts came to mind as you did this?

   • If someone asked you to do their homework for him or her, would you?

   • Have you ever pulled a prank on someone like Mark Twain did?

   • Have you ever gotten one of your friends to help you with a chore?

AFTER THE READER'S THEATER

1. Have the class complete the Question Strips graphic organizer idependently.

2. Then have students work in pairs to answer each other's questions. Remind students to refer back to the script for more information.

3. Have each pair create a poster about Mark Twain. The poster should provide information about his life, personal characteristics, accomplishments, etc. The poster should include both text and illustrations.

RESPONSE QUESTIONS

Group Discussion Questions

   • What kind of a person was Mark Twain? Give three examples from the script to support your answer.

   • Twain loved to read. What types of stories do you like reading?

Written Response Question

   • Do you agree or disagree with the saying "Sticks and stones may break my bones but names can never hurt me"? Explain your answer.

Name_____ Date _____

Question Strips

Who?	_____

What?	_____

When?	_____

Why?	_____

How?	_____

What If?	_____

To Tell the Truth with Mark Twain

BY GAIL SKROBACK HENNESSEY

A reader's theater with seven parts

Host: Today's guest is Mark Twain. Only one of our three guests is the REAL American humorist and writer. The other two on the panel are imposters. Your job is to listen carefully to the information presented and decide which of the three guests is the REAL Mark Twain. Let's begin by meeting our guest.

Twain 1: Good day to you. My name is Samuel Clemens. I am better known as Mark Twain.

Twain 2: Hello! The name is Sam Clemens and I'm glad to be here.

Twain 3: I was born Samuel Clemens, but you can call me Mark Twain.

Host: Let me read this brief summary on Mark Twain. Mark Twain was born Samuel Langhorne Clemens in Florida, Missouri, in 1835. He spent much of his boyhood along the banks of the Mississippi River. At 11, his father died and he had to go to work to support his family. At 21, he boarded a riverboat bound for South America, where he planned to seek his fortune collecting cocoa along the Amazon River. Instead, he decided to become a riverboat pilot. The outbreak of the Civil War ended the riverboat traffic, and he eventually moved to the Nevada Territory. While out west, he began to write and sell his stories. He decided on the pen name Mark Twain, a term meaning two fathoms deep. Many consider Mark Twain to be the best and most popular author of all time. You probably have heard about or read some of his books, such as *Tom Sawyer* and *The Adventures of Huckleberry Finn*. About a year before his death, he said, "I came in with Halley's comet in 1835. It is coming again next year, and I expect to go out with it. It will be the greatest disappointment of my life if I don't go out with Halley's comet." Halley's Comet appeared in 1910 and Mark Twain died that same year, going out with the comet as he wished.

Let's begin the questioning with Panelist 1.

Panelist 1: When you were born, your father was concerned that you were tiny and weak looking. Your mother called your long, slow drawl, "Sammy's long talk," which eventually became one of your trademarks. The Mississippi River attracted your attention at an early age. Can you tell us more about your childhood, Mr. Twain?

To Tell the Truth with Mark Twain *(cont.)*

Twain 1: I guess you could say that I was quite a handful for my parents. As a baby, they often found me heading toward the Mississippi River. One time, I almost drowned before they found me. Yes, I guess you could say the Mississippi River interested me from a very early age! Many of my stories draw on my experiences growing up along the Mississippi.

Twain 2: I remember that my mother was always impressed because I took my medicine so willingly. Little did she know that when she wasn't looking, I poured it down a crack in the dining room floor! I also remember feeling left out when many of the kids at school caught the measles, so I went to visit a kid who had them, hoping that I would catch them. I did!

Twain 3: I loved to explore and one day I brought my mother a present from a cave I had been exploring. I told her to reach into my pant's pocket and pull it out. Ha, Ha, it was a live bat! Another time, I sneaked aboard a riverboat to see what was going on. Unfortunately, I got caught and the pilot threw me off the boat!

Panelist 2: It seems like you liked to play pranks. You tell a story about the time when you put a bunch of snakes in your aunt's sewing basket just to see her reaction. I was wondering, Mr. Twain, what kind of student were you?

Twain 1: I loved learning and was especially interested in science. I had the highest grades in my class, and many classmates would ask me to help them with their homework. I took school very seriously and I never played pranks!

Twain 2: I remember one of my teachers said of me, "Sam's speech may be slow of speech but he's certainly not slow at thinking of ways to get out of studying." Although I did not find much use for most subjects in school, I was very good at spelling bees and I usually won the weekly competitions.

Twain 3: I had difficulty concentrating in class. I was too interested in what was happening outside of the classroom. I got many whippings for my bad school performance. One time, my dad told me to go outside and get a piece of wood for him to use to whip me. I brought back a long curled shaving of wood! Unfortunately, he went out to get a stick.

Panelist 3: You wrote one of your earliest stories, "The Celebrated Jumping Frog of Calaveras County," while working in California for a local newspaper. After it was published, people began to notice your humorous stories and the funny exaggerations you used to tell. Tell us about your books.

To Tell the Truth with Mark Twain *(cont.)*

Twain 1: In *Tom Sawyer*, Tom is ordered to whitewash the back fence, a chore he has been given as a punishment. He pretends to enjoy it so much that he fools the neighbor kids and they pay him for the privilege of whitewashing the fence for him. This really happened to me. Some of the loot I got from the kids included an apple, a kitten, a brass doorknob, and twelve marbles.

Twain 2: My most popular book is *The Adventures of Huckleberry Finn*. It was published in 1884 and translated into more than 50 languages. Even today, more than 200,000 copies are sold each year in the United States. Some people today are critical of the book for its language and others criticize the way African Americans are treated in the story.

Twain 3: In honor of my story, "The Celebrated Jumping Frog of Calaveras County," there is a frog-jumping contest each year at the Calaveras County Fair!

Panelist 1: When you were a boy, the wind blew a page from a book on Joan of Arc at your feet. It was one of the first "books" you had seen and you claim that it introduced you to the wonders of books. (Later in life, you wrote a book on Joan of Arc.) Where did you develop your interest in story telling and where did you get the ideas for your stories?

Twain 1: I always had my head stuck in a book. I loved to read, especially mysteries and adventure stories. I also liked to read stories about space people coming to Earth, such as *My Teacher Is an Alien* and *My Teacher Fried My Brains* by Bruce Coville. The topics for my stories came from my imagination.

Twain 2: Most of the ideas for my stories just popped into my head while I was roller skating down the streets of Hannibal or while I was streaking down the slopes on my snowboard. I thought best in the outdoors where I made up the ideas for my stories.

Twain 3: Books were scarce when I was growing up. I remember that my aunt had some slaves at her home, and I spent many a summer's night listening intently to one slave named Jennie tell stories late into the night. Jennie's stories instilled in me a love of storytelling. My mother also said that I was excellent at pretend games in which I used my imagination to become a pirate, a cowboy, or a bandit. Many of my stories draw on both my experiences as a child and as an adult. For example, in *Tom Sawyer*, Tom does something I did as a boy. My mom forbade me to go swimming in cold weather and sewed up my collar so she could tell if I had disobeyed and gone swimming. I simply took a needle and thread with me to swimming hole, ripped open the collar and then sewed it back up before I went home!

To Tell the Truth with Mark Twain *(cont.)*

Panelist 2: As one of America's greatest humorists, you said many funny things that are famous now. You once said, "Truth is more of a stranger than fiction." You also said," Each person is born with one possession which out values all his others—his last breath" and "Let us save the tomorrows for work." What other comments are you famous for saying?

Twain 1: "Sticks and stones may break my bones but names can never hurt me." Another famous saying of mine is, "Sally sells seashells by the sea shore."

Twain 2: "I came, I saw, I conquered." Another of my quotes, which I am sure you have heard, is, " When in Rome, do as the Romans do."

Twain 3: "Work and play are words used to describe the same thing under differing conditions." I also said, "The man with a new idea is a crank until the idea succeeds."

Panelist 3: As a successful writer and humorist, you were known the world over and must have had a very happy life. Tell us a bit about your life after you became so famous.

Twain 1: My life was great! I was so famous that people always wanted my autograph. I had to wear a wig over my well-known, white bushy hair, and I had to wear dark sunglasses whenever I wanted to go out so I would not be recognized.

Twain 2: Yes, life was good. I appeared on several television shows. I was working on a CD when Halley's comet reappeared and you know what happened then…

Twain 3: Sadly, despite my success, my life was filled with much tragedy. I made bad investments with the money I made from my books and speaking tours and actually went deeply into debt. To pay off my debts, I took a European tour and actually gave lectures using foreign interpreters. While I was in Europe, one of my daughters, Susy, became ill and died. A few years later, my beloved wife, Olivia, died. Five years after her death, my daughter, Jean, died. I spent my last few years alone and very unhappy.

Host: Panelists and members of the audience, it is now time for you to decide whom you think is the real Mark Twain. Is it Twain 1, Twain 2, or Twain 3?

All right, the votes have been cast. Will the REAL Mark Twain please stand up?

References Cited

Kuhn, Melanie R. and Steven A. Stahl. 2000. *Fluency: A review of developmental and remedial practices*. Ann Arbor, MI: Center for the Improvement of Early Reading Achievement.

LaBerge, David and S. Jay Samuels. 1974. Toward a theory of automatic information processing in reading. *Cognitive Psychology* 6: 293–323.

National Reading Panel. 2000. *Teaching children to read: An evidence-based assessment of the scientific research literature on reading and its implications for reading instruction—reports of the subgroups*. Washington, DC: National Institute of Child Health and Human Development.

Rasinski, Timothy. 1990. *The effects of cued phrase boundaries in texts*. Bloomington, IN: ERIC Clearinghouse on Reading and Communication Skills.

Samuels, S. Jay. 1979. The method of repeated reading. *The Reading Teacher* 32: 403–408.

U.S. Department of Education. 2001. *Put Reading First: The Research Building Blocks for Teaching Children to Read*. Washington, DC: U.S. Government Printing Office.

Recommended Children's Literature

Bendrick, Jeanne. *Archimedes and the Door of Science*. Bathgate ND: Bethlehem Books; 1995.

Brooks, Phillip. *Hannibal: Rome's Worst Nightmare*. London: Franklin Watts, 2009.

Dickinson, Emily. *Poems for Youth*. New York: Little Brown & Co., 1996.

Freedman, Russel. *Out of Darkness: The Story of Louis Braille*. New York: Clarion Books,1997.

Henry, Joanne Landers. *Elizabeth Blackwell: Girl Doctor*. New York: Aladdin, 1996.

Herbert, Janis. *Leonardo da Vinci for Kids: His Life and Ideas*. Chicago Review Press: Chicago, IL, 1998.

Langley, Andrew. *Alexander the Great*. New York: Oxford University Press, USA, 1998.

McDonough, Yona Zeldis. *Who Was Harriet Tubman?* New York: Grosset & Dunlap, 2002.

Pastan, Amy. *Gandhi: DK Biography*. New York: DK Children, 2006.

Poe, Edgar Allan. *Edgar Allan Poe's Tales of Mysteries and Madness*. New York: Atheneum, 2004.

Rasmussen, Kent B. *Mark Twain for Kids: His Life and Times*. Chicago Review Press: Chicago, IL, 1998.

Usher, M.D. *Wise Guy: The Life and Philosophy of Socrates*. New York: Farrar, Straus, and Giroux, 2005.

Contents of the
Teacher Resource CD

Script Title	Filename
Socrates	socrates.pdf
Archimedes	archimedes.pdf
Hannibal	hannibal.pdf
Alexander the Great	alexanderthegreat.pdf
Leonardo Da Vinci	leonardodavinci.pdf
Louis Braille	louisbraille.pdf
Elizabeth Blackwell	elizabethblackwell.pdf
Gandhi	gandhi.pdf
Edgar Allan Poe	edgarallanpoe.pdf
Harriet Tubman	harriettubman.pdf
Emily Dickinson	emilydickinson.pdf
Mark Twain	marktwain.pdf
Graphic Organizer	**Filename**
K-W-L Chart	kwlchart.pdf
Fact or Opinion Chart	factoropinion.pdf
Question Strips	questionstrips.pdf
Idear Web	ideaweb.pdf
Box Summary	boxsummary.pdf
Main Idea and Details	mainidea.pdf
Cluster Web	clusterweb.pdf
Sequential Order	sequentialorder.pdf
Outline Form	outlineform.pdf
Attribute Diagram	attributediagram.pdf
Compare and Contrast	compareandcontrast.pdf

Notes

Notes